4

HOME & HEART

HOME *&* HEART

Simple, Beautiful Ways to Create Spirit, Harmony & Warmth in Every Room

BEVERLY PAGRAM

DAYBREAK

Cover Designer: Sara Mathews
Cover Photographer: Andreas von Einsiedel

Library of Congress Cataloging-in-Publication Data
available on request

ISBN 0-87596-522-9

Distributed in the book trade by St. Martin's Press

hardcover

10 9 8 7 6 5 4 3 2 1

DAYBREAK

—— OUR PURPOSE ——
*"We inspire and enable people to improve
their lives and the world around them."*

'More of a poem than a house.'
Dante Gabriel Rossetti, describing Red House,
the home created by William Morris

About This Book

In this book you will be guided through the thought
processes and design-for-living inspiration which will
give you the confidence to take action in a homemaking
program with a difference. In order to move from
'home' as an abstract concept to a special, health-giving
place which both bears our personal stamp and nur-
tures our inner needs, we have to first do some ground-
work. A sense of belonging does not come out of thin
air; it comes from connection with 'family' (either
genetic or chosen), place, reassuringly familiar objects,
and, above all, some sort of belief or value system. This
book does not advocate any particular religious path
but outlines a gentle spiritual enhancement based on
harmony with the the natural world.

Contents

PART 2
Functions for the Home 59

introduction

The concept of `home' occupies a unique place in the sensibilities and affections of all human beings in the global village, whatever their finances or geography. Whether we live in a shack or a palace we retreat from the outside world to our homes not just for physical shelter and refreshment but for inner renewal also. But feeling positive and fulfilled cannot be achieved in a home environment where the senses are deprived and there is impoverishment of the soul.

This book is about making sure our living spaces offer a warm emotional landscape and reflect the individuality of the people who spend so much time in them. That they offer the right psychic climate to generate the sharing, continually learning and caring home-culture which makes happy, healthy children and well-balanced grown-ups. Ways of making this possible are mostly simple. They rest on encouraging personal creativity, satisfying effort and self-expression for everyone in the household; as well as meaningful, security-enhancing daily and seasonal ritual and celebration for individuals and groups. Most important in the home sanctuary is the concept of 'bringing the outside in' and 'taking the inside out' – an environmental shift in lifestyle-thinking, setting everyday lives in harmony with the natural world.

As we hover around the cusp of the millennium, many of us feel a sense of alienation from the polluting, throwaway society which is devouring the planet. We feel that the pace of life is way too fast – for many of us relaxation equals gulping down an unhealthy carry-out meal in front of some banal late night TV. We suffer from technology overload, and fear that in the public eye we are defined only by our purchases. People who feel like this and yearn for a different, calmer lifestyle will hopefully find this book a helpful *aide-mémoire* and ideas bank in their quest to give their homes *genius loci* – spirit of place.

Essence of the Divine

The spirit referred to is an intangible ingredient that has nothing to do with any particular religious path, but everything to do with unfettered imagination, and a sense of the sacred. The latter can of course be found aplenty in places designated divine for centuries, such as Chartres Cathedral, in France, or the Shwedagon Buddhist temple complex in Burma. It can also be found everywhere in nature, and many people bring back this essence stored in their memories from beach and country holidays: a shell or collection of pressed flowers serving as a simple visual metaphor for a fleeting moment of communion with the living processes of the biosphere.

This book is therefore about finding or conjuring that nature-reverent warmth and ecological 'sacredness' in our homes, and how to enhance and enjoy this revelational sense of extended selfhood in a new vibrant way. It is concerned not only with things authentic, healthy, creative, and soundly eco but also with that much-suppressed universal mystic aspect of the human ego that craves serenity, introspection, and a greater understanding of the whys and wherefores of the cosmos.

In many countries people have looked for explanations for the mysteries of life and the universe in fascinating signs, images, and symbols they consider imbued with meaning. These often esthetically enchanting tokens and illustrations crop up in many different traditions. Consider the uncanny similarity between the Shaker and Amish cut-paper hand-shaped 'blessings' motif and the filigree good luck hand symbol drawn on exterior house walls in rural India, North Africa, and the Middle East.

Plainness and Simplicity

Mother Ann Lee, spiritual founder of the Shaker movement in New England in 1774, encapsulated the homely 'holiness' of her house and garden in her request that 'whatever is fashioned, let it be plain and simple and for the good'. This home-based honesty is worth adopting – we can capture its essence by our choice and use of natural nontoxic paint and fabrics; beautiful and durable wood and stone; energy-efficient heating, cooking, and lighting; and appetizing organically produced food. Those not drawn to monastic and minimalist lifestyles can add warmth and 'heart' to their homes with interesting found objects and culturally diverse possessions: furniture, ornaments, images, and eclectic accessories to create a vivid kaleidoscope of color and context.

Creative Cavalcade

The cavalcade of creative people in the past who have espoused a nature-harmonious 'organic' ethos and a sense of place and form in their work and lifestyles include pioneering American architect Frank Lloyd Wright; Austrian anthroposophist philosopher Rudolf Steiner, who proposed that people's immediate physical home environment shaped their future emotions and approach to life; Victorian English poet/artist/political activist William Morris and friends in the Arts and Crafts movement; and Spanish architect Antonio Gaudí whose exuberant free-flowing buildings are now a major Barcelonan tourist attraction.

The banner is still being flown by, among many others, the contemporary American, Scandinavian, and European designers whose creed of 'building biology' creates structures based on a health-giving holistic relationship beween man and the living environment.

Some women artists, notably Mexico-based surrealists Frida Kahlo and Remedios Varo, explored the links between nature and magic, folklore, mysticism, and mythology, both in their art and habitat. Both were recorders of dreams, collectors of stones, shells, and crystals, and believers in the ritual placement of these 'sacred' objects in their homes and gardens.

The delightfully contradictory grace and rusticity of contemporary Scandinavian interior design owes much to Swedish artist Carl Larsson and his textile designer wife Karin. At the end of the notoriously stuffy nineteenth century the couple created an Arcadian idyll in and around their home, Lilla Hyttnas. In this highly functional Utopia simple utilitarian craftsmanship was married with 'childish' fantasy paint-effects including ornamental mottoes and flowing fairytale script … and everywhere, artless vases and jam jars of flowers and herbs.

Lifestory Narrative

Each room in your house and each area of your garden can be a canvas on which you can paint a lifestory narrative. Display unusual and/or 'meaningful' ornaments, tactile natural objects, and photographs and/or pictures which to you are inner-life map markers. Encourage other family members to do the same with artefacts and art which are special, magical, or symbolically important to them. By the same token, let your home have a say in its look! Let its intrinsic character and style lead your decoration, and remember that even the supposedly 'characterless' new dwelling has something positive to be devel-

oped and enhanced, be it wonderful natural light or a tiny slice of a kitchen evoking a ship's narrow cooking galley.

There is something very satisfying in giving a junkshop purchase a new lease of life, or making something out of a found object. When we create something new and exciting out of a silvery piece of driftwood or a rickety old abandoned chest of drawers we feel as if we are both being thrifty with the environment's resources and tapping into an historical continuum.

If we are not lucky enough to inherit heirlooms, then we can invent our own from found or junk-store artifacts with a patina of age. And after all, every picture or article of furniture we paint or make will (hopefully!) one day amuse and/or delight our children and grandchildren.

A sense of welcome and 'heart' is an elusive quality which some homes seem to have aplenty, and others, despite their expensive but severe ambient lighting, fashionable furniture, and deep-pile carpets, miss by miles. A home, after all, should not be a 'dream house', for that implies the limits of a dull, finished perfection. Your living space, however, is a place which will develop and change as you and your partner/family learn new things and rediscover old yearnings. With its ongoing sense of wonder, and concentration on well-being, it should become an abode to dream in. This book shows you how to arrange your house so that you have personal time and place to do just that.

However, despite most people's undoubted need for contemplation, there must also be lots of time windows opened for the purposes of conviviality and expanding the potential of relationships. It is well known that friends old and new seem to flock where they can sit cozily in the kitchen with a glass of wine and talk to the cook! Increasing numbers of guests shun the formal dinner party and prefer to eat at the candle-lit kitchen table off interesting mismatched plates. Other essential ingredients in the people-magnetic house are plentiful and wholesome food and lively conversation, where a good balance of laughter and world issues get more airtime than the energy-sapping 'inwardness' of TV or therapy updates.

Ceremonial Set Dressing

A sense of theater is undoubtedly useful when there is a gathering, however casual the occasion. Even the most sophisticated folk display childlike appreciation when effort is put into a bit of ceremonial set-dressing. This can be as simple as using a multi-hued, mirrored sari for a tablecloth when serving a curry or turning large seasonal leaves into temporary placemats.

The successful evocation of mood, time, and place is usually a subtle assault on all the senses and energies at once. This book shows how different relaxing, healing, and uplifting atmospheres can be created – with, for example, unusual blends of aromatics, sensitive lighting, and sound effects, and a romantic, visionary use of color and texture. Perhaps the most important factor of all, however, in creating your own Eden, is 'bringing the outside in'. Oriental, Middle Eastern, and Mediterranean peoples have been doing this for many centuries with their concept of the urban inner courtyard garden, which often just affords the passerby a tantalizing glimpse of green fronds and splashing water through a half-open doorway in a busy, dusty street.

Many cultures include daily small household rituals of thanksgiving for the bounty of nature. When we put a bunch of flowers in a jar or vase on the kitchen table we are taking part in an ancient 'sacred' custom which knows no geographical boundaries. 'Bringing the outside in' can be as simple as having a jungle of eco-friendly, visually arresting, houseplants on the windowsill. Having a 'garden' in every room provides a variety of microclimates as well as a microcosm of the natural world. By also 'taking the inside out' people extend the dimensions of their living space by socializing, working, and meditating outside. Here, admiring the moon and stars by candlelight or having a solitary think while watering the plants so venerated and mythologized by our ancestors, we are perhaps most open in our psychic consciousness. Certainly we are most aware of the power and mystery of the elements.

PART 1

Foundations for the Heart

Foundations for the Heart

Foundations for the Heart gives an ecological, cultural, and sensory frame of reference to our home environment, and briefly outlines some of the practical things we can do to bring 'heart' to it. Chapter One, Elements, explains how earth, fire, water, and air work together in harmony and balance, their symbolic value in many cultures, and how to discover new ways of using, visualizing, and appreciating them in our homes. Chapter Two, Seasons, is a fresh-look inventory of the atmospheric attributes of the seasons, their mythology, and the multicultural festivals which have celebrated them through the centuries and are due for a revival ... perhaps in your home. Chapter Three, Sensations, looks at everything to do with seeing, hearing, smelling, and touching. You indulge your curiosity and stretch your powers of observation to explore inspiring new and old sensibilities that can transform and expand the dimensions of your living space.

elements

Throughout human history, the four elements, earth, fire, air, and water, have played a paramount role in our physical and spiritual lives. When survival depended on an intimate relationship with the natural world, reverence for all its component parts provided a continual state of grace for our species. Our ancestors deified the landscape, and the mighty forces of earth, wind, water, and fire that shaped it. So evolved the celestial element-beings – the kachina sun god of the Pueblo Indians, the Greek nymph-caretakers of the waters, the Polynesian atua weather spirits, the Japanese mountain/volcano god O-Yama-Tsu-Mi.

Sense of Wonder

These days, people concerned with planetary environmental issues, and developing ecologically healthy housing, are often interested in recultivating the sense of wonder felt by our forefathers toward nature's primordial forces. In great ancient cities, such as Knossos on the Greek island of Crete, the concepts of home comfort and elemental veneration were as one. The colonnaded courtyards of the royal palace were decorated with frescoes of the earth goddess Rhea and her spiral symbol in vivid red and blue mineral pastes. Near by, Minoan courtiers frolicked in seawater pools lined with glittering mosaics of sacred fish and flowers.

Incorporating ideas from ethnic housing can help balance the physical and spiritual needs in your home. The most enduring vernacular design materials and techniques are so simple and versatile. For example, the elegant rattan and bamboo stilt houses (with integral front veranda) of Indonesia and Malaysia; the much-embellished sculptural mud buildings of Tunisia with their rabbit-warren of cool inner rooms; and the monumental rough-hewn log and stone cabins of North America and Scandinavia.

Mix-and-match borrowing that is *ad hoc* and multicultural marries pared-down essentials, such as natural materials that give shelter or invite heat or cold, to a variety of traditional crafts with folkloric/mythical overtones.

Rich Resources

Elementals like wood and stone look their most mysterious and atmospheric when eroded, patterned, pitted, smoothed, or faded by other elements. Whether we choose radiant or dustily subtle organic paint pigments, lacily filigreed wooden shutters, or a thatched stone turret, we are tapping in to a rich international channel of resources to make our homes refuges of tranquility, creative endeavor, and 'green' ethos and ethics.

Being in touch with all the elements engages our senses, sensualities, and sensibilities. We become more tactile, more observant of natural shape and form, and more aware of the wide variety of life-forms that exist in earth, air, and water. With this new awareness comes interest in imaginative low-tech, 'bio-climatic' buildings, and sustainable lifestyles making the most of sun, wind, and water power for energy and inspiration.

Relationship With the Earth

The human need to have a close relationship with the Earth in many places in the world takes a dramatically literal, utilitarian form. Around half the world's houses are actually built of mud, which when dried and made into bricks, provides won-derful insulation. Some buildings, in Europe and China, have robust-ly lasted ever since medieval times. The rugged grandeur of the classic Spanish colonial adobe buildings of unbaked, sun-dried earth and straw bricks in New Mexico, as well as the traditional sculptured cellular 'beehive' baked clay dwellings of some Indian and African peoples, have inspired many contemporary ecologically ori-ented architects and builders to start using ordi-nary, humble earth as a serious creative building medium once more.

Nowhere does the human need to be `ground-ed' by an intimate relationship with the earthscape manifest itself more strongly than in 'The Dreaming', the mythic creation time-span of the Australian Aboriginal people.

Seeking a natural 'burrow' blessed with spiritual protection by the earth spirits, many peoples of the past have used caves as dwellings and shelters. Our memorials to our dead (tumuli, pyramids), as well as our places of worship (stupas, ziggurats, cathedral spires), echo our innate reverence for mounds and mountains. Buddhist teachings describe the pointed, four-sided stupa, with the all-seeing eye painted on to each face, as 'the being as one with the uni-versal spirit'. Nomadic Native Americans have always shared this passionate primal feeling of the *anima mundi*, or world soul. The peoples of the Pacific coast of Canada collected special 'spirit stones' from certain beaches and painted them with hieroglyphs to attract protection.

Collecting Crystals

Many people also collect earth crystals and gemstones both for their physical beauty as decorative objects and for their strongly positive effect on the seven chakras (centers of vibrational energy) they believe operate within the human body. Having crystals in the house – either hanging in windows as prisms catching light, or resting in small bowls where they shimmer by can-dlelight, one taps in to an ancient tradition of rev-erence for the innate 'magic' of earth's minerals.

Linked in international arcane lore to specific stars, planets, and zodiac images, gems have been used since earliest times in talismans and charms.

A beryl, for example, was considered a stone of prophecy under the dominion of Venus in medieval England; an unblemished quartz crystal was a mystical healing stone in many cultures from South America to Japan.

'Bringing the outside in' makes the demarcation between our homes and the physical elements of nature less rigid. It can be as simple a gesture as displaying a collection of particularly beautiful and/or unusual rocks and pebbles in a surprising decorative context – heaped, say, with huge rugged balls of string, onions, fresh figs, or old glass fishing buoys.

The spiral, a symbol of power and creativity, was widely used on wall and floor tiles in the ancient world. Tiles of baked or sun-dried earth, glazed and unglazed, plain or spectacularly decorated, adorned the floors and walls of rich and poor alike since before the time of the Pharaohs. Terracotta – meaning literally 'baked earth', with its rich, rusty, and nut-brown hues – is still an elegant and practical choice for people who want their homes to combine a sunny, country appeal with tactile pleasure – walking barefoot on earth tiles in the sun is an unforgettably warm, sensory feeling. The random crackle-glazing on some wall and floor tiles, and indeed on raku-style earthenware pottery, recalls the cracks and splits on hard-baked desert earthscapes.

Positive energies can certainly be very effectively conjured in your rooms by the use of eco-friendly, earth-colored paint pigments, from deep chocolate browns through the glowing red and ocher-yellow spectrums to the Siena-pink chalkiness of raw plaster and luminous clay-look of limewash. Wood has always been a favorite building and furniture material in all civilizations, as it uniquely lends itself to both intricate carving and painting. Driftwood is a very evocative 'spiritual' medium from which to create picture-frames, chairs, and tables; for it contains not only the intrinsic form and essence of the living tree but also the wave-caressed surface grain, evidence of gradual transformation by the ocean.

Observing Seasonal Change

Change, seasonal and in growth, is a continual pleasurable theme to be observed by anyone in possession of a few pots of earth and some plant and tree seedlings. By opening the windows wide, by stepping over the doorstep on to the patio to smell the rain-freshened earth, by bringing trees to live indoors – we can observe and feel the nurture, harmonies, rhythms, and fertility of the Earth first hand.

In this magical realm, with the right sensibilities of delight and contentment, we can create a mini rainforest or a paradise garden to cherish, giving our dreams actual dimensions. There is no greater homage we can pay Gaia than to work with our hands in her rich earth, assisting in the alchemy of the greening process.

earth

'The earth provides all things,
And receives all again.'
Old American proverb

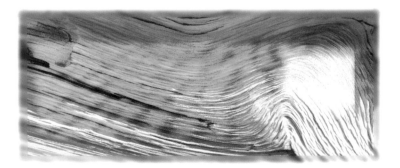

f i r e

'He who is in the fire, and He who is in
the Heat, and He who is in the Sun, are
all one and the same.'
The Upanishads

'What is the odds as long as the fire of soul is
kindled at the taper of conwiviality ...'
The Old Curiosity Shop, Charles Dickens, 1841

21

Ever since we discovered how to create flame from friction, fire has been considered a sacred gift. Everything to do with fire-making has been steeped in magic and ritual, from the sort of wood burned to divinations from the shape of flames and cinders, and supernatural messages in the smoke. Our word 'focus' comes from the Latin for hearth, and in early times in Europe the hearth was indeed in the center of the one room of the house, with the smoke sharing the entrance and exit hole – access by ladder only. Fire's sheer energy and remarkable powers of transformation made it the centerpiece of many divinatory and ceremonial rituals. It has also always symbolized social cohesion – the fire was where the family group gathered. And the greatest gift bestowed on those starting their own family was firebrands from the ancestral hearth. In ancient times the Greek goddess Hestia presided over the family hearth, whose matriarch gave offerings to the goddess via the flames. The Romans instituted a religious 'public' hearth in a temple in Rome, tended day and night by the 'Vestal Virgins', dedi-

cated to the goddess Vesta. They believed that this fire was the center of the universe, and that to let it go out spelled disaster.

Fire Lore and Festivals

For the Celts in Europe, the great seasonal fire festivals of Imbolc, Beltane, Lammas, and Samhain were times of renewal and celebration, when the sacred 'need-fire' was carried home from the ceremonial blaze to re-kindle the wood on the family hearth and thereby offer cosmic protection to all who sat around it.

Strict rules governed who handled the fire-tongs and poker – strangers were often forbidden to touch them unless they had known the family for a number of years. The metal 'fire dogs' the logs rested on in European and early American homes, were always made of iron, a metal legendarily associated with protection against fairy spells; the stylized 'dogs' represented fierce fireside hounds guarding flames and family alike.

Iron horse-shoes were often nailed on to the fireplace beam as luck-bringers alongside carved runes, little crosses made of mystical rowan-wood, and votive supplications or thanksgiving notes scored on metal. Small wonder, then, that in many homes the mantelpiece has come to resemble a sort of secular 'altar', arrayed with family photographs, social invitations, candles, and small special ornaments and evocative found objects.

Though we may feel nostalgic for the crackle of burning logs, open fires are inefficient heaters (more than eighty percent of the energy goes up the chimney). They also pollute the indoor atmosphere and contribute to the buildup of greenhouse gases in the environment at large. If you *do* have an open fire, make sure adequate air comes into the room to carry the smoke up the chimney. A delightful way of perfuming a room and banishing next day's smell of old soot and smoke is to burn aromatic woods like hickory and lilac, as well as dried citrus peels, juniper berries, and kindling subtly scented with spicy essential oils such as cinnamon and sandalwood. Because the hearth is so important as a nurturing focal point in a family living space (a focus unfortunately often usurped by that rival 'eye' the television), we need to re-think how we use it. Perhaps we could combine ancient custom and modern technology by installing a high-performance combustion stove. Many have glass doors so that the glow of the fire can still be enjoyed. Traditional in the Netherlands, Germany, Russia, and Scandinavia for at least five centuries, they are ornately tiled and pillar-shaped.

Few of us are lucky enough to possess an inglenook seat actually inside the fireplace itself, where one can sit and watch the smoke wafting up the chimney; but we can provide cozy, squashy sofas, big fat pillows, or a custom-built semi-circular seating platform. Here, friends and family can feel at the heart of the house; they can chat and reminisce, or just stare at the embers and think and wonder in a spirit of community and well-being. This is also a favorite snoozing place for animals to feel secure and comfy, and to dream. A warm, deep pillow or basket near the fire/stove will give your dog or cat a great deal of dozing joy. In the past, the hearth was a means of cooking food. In medieval Europe pots were hung by the side of the hearth blaze on an iron trivet, while some fire-dogs had little cups set in their heads for people to warm their drinks. Although few of us

want to return permanently to the primitive cooking conditions of those days, it is atmospheric on special occasions to perform a few antique culinary feats. Bread and potatoes can be cooked in the ashes; chestnuts and sweet Bur Oak acorns (much favored by the Canadian Chippewa peo-

ple), roasted on special pierced pans (or ordinary shovels); toast, muffins, and marshmallows dangled on forks until sufficiently crispy. Spiced mulled wine always tastes richer when warmed in a pan over the embers.

Candle Lighting

Lighting candles is a miniature fire-making ritual that everyone enjoys. This illuminating symbol of life can be conjured inside and out by lighting: the Jewish menora; the many-branched Greek Orthodox church candlestick thronged with beeswax *candili*; the French terra-cotta outdoor candlepot; the old colonial storm lantern; Buddhist lamasery temple tapers; a dish swimming with glimmering nightlights … it matters not what sort, the primeval pleasure, the sense that here is truly an awesome gift from the gods, is always present. And reflecting the flames in water or mirrors increases their magical impact.

Almost three-quarters of the Earth's surface is covered with water, its topography slowly but dramatically carved by this forceful element into peaks and ravines. But of the liquid vastness, alas only one percent is freshwater – and without this quixotic transforming component, our planet could sustain no life. Like the Earth, our bodies are also about seventy percent water. Not only do we need plentiful supplies of this veritable elixir of life to physically survive we also need it to cleanse ourselves, our food, our possessions. It is no surprise then that since the very earliest times the sound, feel, and look that water has to humanity have also represented spiritual refreshment. And that lakes, seas, rivers, and wells have been considered meaningful, holy, and prophetic in all cultures. This valuable primordial fluid, therefore, plays a highly significant role in many religious cults and rituals around the globe as a representation of both godly purity and cosmic life itself.

Many people feel emotionally 'linked' to water, perhaps because of a vestigial memory of floating safely and peacefully in the womb. They feel moved by the sight and sound of the untameable seas and oceans. Small wonder, then, that in many cultures deep water symbolizes the subconscious mind, and that individuals the world over feel the need to recreate in their backyards the unique harmony of repose and invigoration that a natural water feature provides.

Water flowed in channels through the Hanging Gardens of Babylon both for irrigation and as a symbol of the creative flow from paradise which in their mythology first animated the world. Chinese tradition holds that fast-moving water contains the life force (known as *ch'i*); thus the Chinese liking for small waterfalls in unlikely domestic environments. In superbly symmetrical Persian courtly gardens and dusty desert oases alike the 'fountains of running water' associated in the Qu'uran with Eden were recreated as an intimation of the bliss to come in the hereafter; while in medieval Europe ornamental wellheads embodied celestial wisdom.

Water Gardens

Japanese Zen Buddhist gardens represent moving water by making innumerable wavelike gradations of dry raked gravel `sea'. Far easier to emulate in our household settings, and also more informal and user-friendly, is the quietly atmospheric Japanese still water garden. The reflective qualities of still water are much utilized as an echo of the divine in Japanese courtyards – where little water bowls are positioned along pathways, both to revive the strolling visitor and to encircle for them a perfect image of the sky.

Water's fascination stems in part from the many forms it can take. As a sheet of water, as well as its weather systems of clouds, mist, rain, ice, and snow, it can be both tranquil and terrifying in quick succession. This ever-changing and unpredictable quality has added to its aura of mystery, and makes water-watching one of mankind's favorite and most rewarding occupations. It undeniably adds to our feeling of at-one-ness with nature to wander in our backyards in the drizzle, observing rain forming tiny pools on the leaves of plants; to watch the formation of complex, beautiful ice crystals on the outside of the windowpane.

Adding magical, silvery water to our enclosed outside living space turns it into a harbor or an oasis. Utilizing it indoors in bowls, decorative pools, or fountains; or rills and channels coursing through the wall from outside – literally `brings the outside in'. It not only provides welcome humidity but establishes a perfect background for daydreaming and meditation. Communing with the water element is stress-busting; and communing with water's fishy inhabitants doubly so. In this new age of aquariums, piscine housing is getting more imaginative and *objet d'art*-oriented as well as more fish-friendly. Some tanks have convex lenses incorporated so that inhabitants can be closely observed.

Water Symbols

Almost any water-related symbol you might choose as a decoration in your home is deeply imbued with historical or legendary significance. 'Sacred geometry' is the term given to the belief system which claims that particular geometric shapes have subtle power over our unconscious minds. In this creed of powerful symbolic abstraction, utilized by the builders of the pyramids and the Parthenon, water is represented by a downward-pointing triangle. This 'feminine' shape was believed by the ancients to hold the mysterious, elusive, fertile spirit of water, and was personified by mythological nymphs, as well as the inverse triangle shape of the mermaid of legend.

The mundane daily rituals of washing and bathing are as important to our sense of emotional well-being as to our physical need for cleansing. They are based in ancient intuitive wisdoms and lore. Aboriginal people in outback Australia dance in the rain when it finally comes after many months of ritual prayers and songs to the Wandjinas, the sacred weather spirits who feature in their cave paintings. Christians baptize in `blessed' water, while in India at Varanasi, devotees gather beside the 'Mother Ganga' to bathe in her and honor her.

Water deserves our respect, for on it our very existences depend. We can all help protect its purity by not pouring toxic products down the drain; and by countering existing pollutants, such as metals and nitrates, with water-filter jugs and faucet filters. Conservation can be as simple as collecting rainwater and dishwater for watering the garden, planting drought-resistant greenery, and fixing leaky faucets and taps.

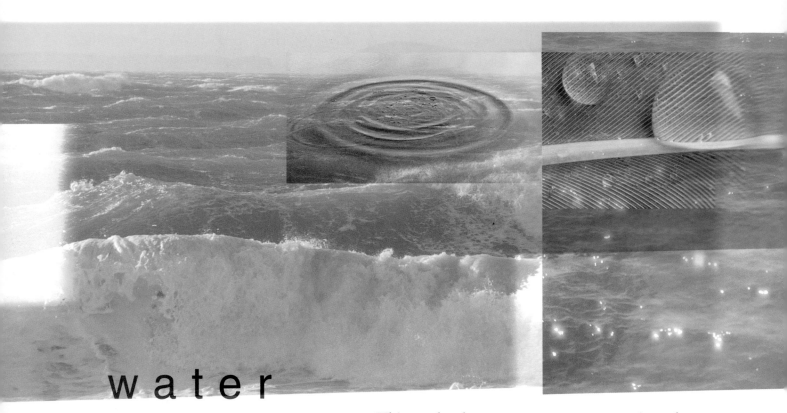

water

*'This used to be among my prayers – a piece of
land not so very large, which would contain a
garden, and near the house a spring of ever-
flowing water.'*
Horace, a Roman poet

*'In the beginning there was only darkness
and emptiness ... there was a warmth, and a
dampness and a soft breathing. The breathing
became a whisper and the whisper grew until it filled
all the space. The first word created "Om". The first
word had power. It created a deep ocean and in the
depths of the ocean lay a seed.'*
Hindu creation myth

26

air

'To thee, whose temple is all space,
Whose altar, earth, sea, skies,
One chorus let all being raise;
All nature's incense rise.'
Alexander Pope

Air, being invisible, is the element most taken for granted. Yet without its oxygen living things would not last more than a few minutes, and without its nitrogen, plants could not grow. Breathing air strongly and deeply is as essential for spiritual well-being as it is for physical health. Air, too, often represents space, the sky, the heavens, the universe, and the cosmos in all their eternity. Here reside the unknowable and the infinite, gods and goddesses, astrological and mythological characters, religious entities, and ideograms. When we stargaze, for astronomical or meditative purposes – or for no reason at all, we look at the very essence of many belief systems.

Real air, the air we breathe when the pressure is right, only rises up to about 30 miles into the atmosphere. Though this air is losing its freshness and cleanliness, we can take action to both protect ourselves from air pollution and contribute in some small way to regenerating the health of the planet.

Many of us spend around ninety percent of our time indoors, and if we ignore the dangers of not only dust-borne bacteria but household chemicals and synthetic furnishings and finishes, we could be contributing to our own and our family's tendency to allergies, hay fever, eczema, and asthma. By choosing organic paints, sealers, primers, and preservatives made of natural resins and plant oils or milk-based casein; and biodegradable, nonenvironmentally hazardous polishes, fresheners, and cleaners we help to make personal air-space pleasant and healthy.

Natural Ventilation

Air quality indoors can also be improved dramatically – initially by providing adequate natural ventilation, which is easier in a home made of porous natural materials such as timber, stone, plaster, and brick because the air diffuses through them. Even in the winter you should make sure that there are some windows open when you are in the house.

The wind and breeze carry sounds and scents from the elements and the seasons, keeping you in touch with the natural world outside – and surely there are few things more romantic than sheer curtains billowing gently in a sudden current of clean, fresh air? Sealed, 'airtight', buildings whose temperature and air quality are provided only by energy-devouring air-conditioning systems are often filled with recycled, stale, bacteria-filled air. Some people use portable and affordable air-filter units to absorb dust, vapors, and other pollutants.

Also, anxious that electrical fields from computer monitors, the static from synthetic materials, televisions, and the like are upsetting the balance between positive and negative ions in the air, the same concerned householders use an ionizer, or negative ion generator, to provide a surfeit of beneficial negative ions that contribute to a sense of well-being. Around half a dozen houseplants in each room can significantly increase air quality by trapping dust in their leaves, and unwelcome vapors in the soil. They can also take the place of a commercial room humidifier, as they add oxygen and humidity to the air.

Natural Perfumes

The scent of plants and flowers also provide a pleasurable enhancement of air quality, for the smell receptors of the human brain, the olfactory nerves, are extremely sensitive.

The word perfume (from the Latin *per fumum*) actually means 'through smoke'. Aromatic woods, gums, and resins in the form of incense sticks and cones have been part of religious ritual since antiquity – the smoke, it was believed, carried the supplications of the worshipers to the deity. Incense smoke has represented the ethereal world at the altars of Osiris, Vishnu, the Buddha, and Jesus alike, and has also been an essential part of the household blessing rituals of countless human beings down the centuries.

Easily available incense sticks and cones in many fragrances enable us to give each room its own ambient perfume mood to suit our emotional needs – from spicy, warm vanilla to sensual amber and subtle, reflective rose. Firewood smoke can also be richly fragrant and atmospheric (albeit polluting!): ash wood smells strange and mystical; lilac and cherry pungent and sweet; heady juniper

much used in pyramidical Tibetan incense altars. In Native American tradition firewood or 'smudging' smoke is wafted with a feather, symbolic of the spirit of air and freedom.

In Ladakh, Tibet, and Nepal people festoon prayer-flags high up in the mountains to catch the winds; similarly women in parts of rural Europe used to tie 'wishes' (written on rags, or, more rarely, paper) on 'sacred' trees growing near rivers or wells believed to be holy. We can follow suit and catch the wind and breezes by decking a small tree with wish-flags. When choosing your tree, remember that the laurel, bay, banyan, peepul, fig, and ash have all been particularly venerated as `cosmic trees'. We can best observe air, the element of change, in all its powerfully moody manifestations – if we give it enough toys to play with. Windmills are a sound, sustainable energy source now being explored on a commercial wind-farm scale. Wind socks, wind-chimes, kites, bunting, pennants, weather-vanes, parasols – these flutter, dance, and turn to remind us of the unseen presence of this alchemic element.

Such mindfulness of air can become a major part of your life, particularly if you spend a few minutes each day focusing on your breathing. Good posture and total quiet are important for conscious and unconscious mind to fuse in a peaceful whole until you experience a oneness with the air.

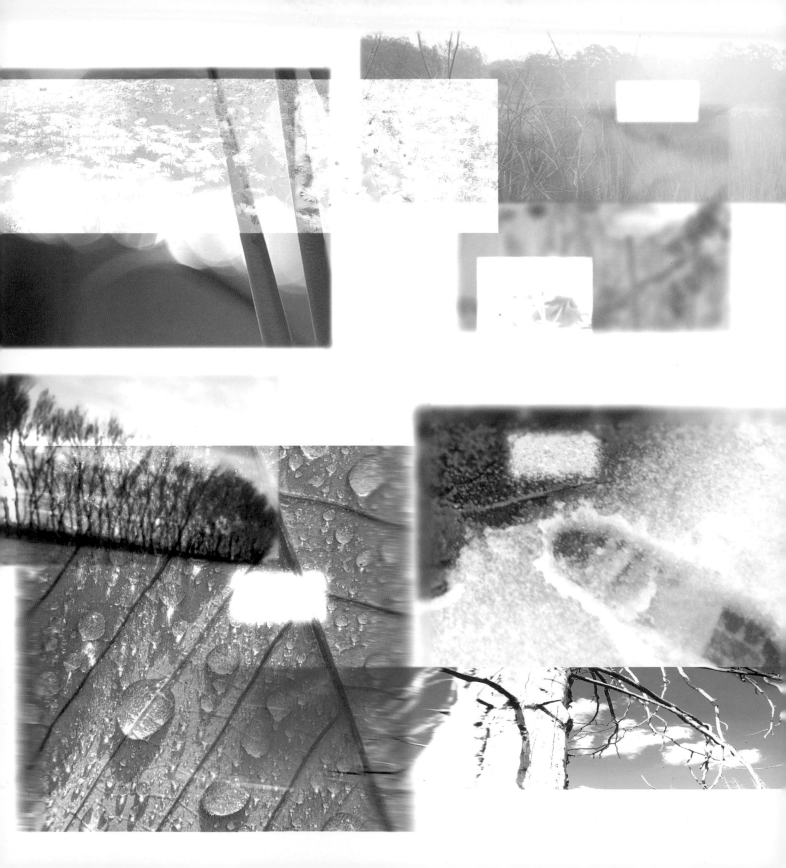

s e a s o n s

When most of our rural-dwelling ancestors lived on the land, they could not have survived if they had not worked in harmony with the cycles of the seasons. Keen observation of the minute signs of imminent weather change that heralded a threat to crops or a new developmental stage in local flora and fauna, often meant the difference between a full belly and an empty larder. In the frenetic modern world, where we rely on the supermarket for our food supply and the flick of an electrical switch for control over light and temperature, it is often difficult to see the yearly calendar as anything other than a convenient adminstrative marker for work and rest periods, and a reminder for birthdays of friends and family.

Losing Touch

Yet once the calendar was a time-measure linked inextricably with the seasonal changes in the natural world, the movement of celestial bodies, and a complex catalog of religious festivals. In gradually losing touch with the seasons we not only alienate ourselves from the beautiful and subtle rhythms and patterns of nature but we are also ignoring our fascinating heritage of associated feasts, fairs, and holy-days. These traditional revels and observations, whatever the contemporary cultural and religious inter-

pretation, often have an ancient pagan, animist origin involving tree, sky, and crop worship.

In a high-tech, increasingly bureaucratic, Western world where ordinary people often feel it is difficult, if not impossible, to maintain control over their lives, 'reclaiming' the seasons, and being aware of the way in which people throughout the global village celebrate them, goes a long way to restoring both a simple sense of local identity and a feeling of oneness with the complex spiritual storybook of humanity.

Many of our Western seasonal festivals were, as they still are in many other parts of the 'undeveloped' world, time-markers when we celebrated our humble thanksgiving for the Earth's past and present fertility, and offered prayers for the continuation of her bounty in the future.

Calendar Systems

Around the world the passing of the year in calendar terms is based on three different systems: the lunar, lunisolar, and solar, which are based on the moon's phases and perceived movements of the sun. Our current Western calendar uses features of the old Roman and Egyptian calendars, and is confusingly based on the solar year, the moon's phases, and the vernal (spring) equinox. Some people prefer to map the passing of the seasons by observing the night sky and the metamorphosing mysterious disc of the moon, personified by Japanese Buddhists as Gwaten; the Ancient Greeks as Hecate and Selene; the Babylonians as Ishtar; the Inca as Mama Quila; and the Pueblo as Yellow Woman. Native Americans have always been keen watchers of the stars – for the Pawnee the Pleiades are both guides and emblems of tribal togetherness. Others invest the planets Mercury, Venus, Mars, Jupiter, Saturn, and their zodiac path through the sky against the constellations with dramatic powers of influence over our lives. They would not dream of planning any month-by-month activity without first consulting their astrological chart.

A Physical Reminder

The easiest way to remind ourselves, especially if we live or work in a high-rise urban space, of the physically changing year, is to bring in each week some seasonal wild or cultivated plants (e.g. flowers, seedpods, gourds). Use them on mantelpieces, tables, shelves, even on the staircase. Vegetables and flowers can be mixed simply together with dramatic effect: artichokes, thistles, and roses; onion flowers and peonies; ornamental cabbages, ivy, and Chinese gooseberry; sunflowers, sage, and runner beans.

Bring the outside in for visual inspiration: papery hydrangea bracts look ethereal combined with the silvery moonlike seed heads of honesty (Lunaria); lavender, seaholly, and eucalypts are similarly other-worldly. Learn the mysterious Victorian symbolic 'language' of flowers; Queen Anne's lace represents 'divine beauty', 'for example; the daisy means 'innocence'; while peach blossom declares: 'your qualities are unequaled'.

Seasonal fruit, whether picked in the garden or bought from the market, looks and smells evocative heaped in colorful bowls: small hard fall apples and chestnuts; red currants and cherries; figs and peaches; oranges, shiny gourds, squashes, and pumpkins. Choose colors and shapes that complement each other and arrange them reverently as works of art, as your very own still lifes. Seasonal herbs and flowers, barks, shells, and stones are unusual, highly individualistic, table decorations at festival meals, on picnics, and for everyday table-settings. A way to make your weekend guests feel special is to place a seasonal decoration or flower arrangement in their room – as simple and unpretentious as a Michaelmas daisy in a jam jar or a few violets in an egg cup.

The Nature Table

Grown-ups and children alike enjoy making seasonal mini nature tables adorned with the summer's precious beachcombing finds, pine cones, abandoned birds' nests, twigs and catkins, fall leaves, pressed wild flowers, pictures of ice crystals, jars of berries and ripened pods, feathers, ears of corn, sheep's wool, a dish of filmy green weed and water-bugs, a butterfly chrysalis, or an ammonite.

With a little imagination some of these finds can be transformed into magical toys and treats. A walnut shell, a small stick, and a leaf or feather made into a fairy's boat; thin flat colored pebbles or limpet shells drilled to make buttons for a special vest; buckeyes threaded together with bright beads to make a necklace.

Our own personal Eden, the garden, is perhaps the place where we best observe the seasonal passing of the year and the growth rhythms of nature. Even in countries such as Australia, where few of the native trees are deciduous and the climatic change through the year not dramatic – the seasons can be subtly beautiful in their variety. The perfumed spring flowers of the silver gum, the smooth, gleaming bark of the shining gum against a gray winter sky; the spring carpets of papery everlastings and the romantic shapes and vivid colors of the kangaroo paws against the spiny grasses – all have enigmatic allure and mystique.

Garden Esthetics

The garden is the place to appreciate the sensuality of lush summer growth and the spare angularity of bare trees and shrubs in winter. In the esthetic winter garden the unusual outlines of denuded vegetation such as corkscrew hazels and weeping willows can provide a starkly sculptural landscape. This stark skeletal quality can be echoed by a homemade twisted wire sculpture, or a mobile of bleached, bonelike branches. Hang small bells on your branches, or strips of silken 'prayer' rags in the tradition of Tibetan Buddhists and Celtic holy women. A favorite meditation spot with a powerful sense of place can become a personal 'shrine' for honoring the passing of the year with an offering of seasonal leaves, flowers, or berries floating (or preserved in ice!) in a dish. Just as the seasonal garden provides repose for both body and mind, so we gain enjoyment and comfort from utilizing nature's bounty in the house. Watch how in the winter, the kitchen seems your home's living heart: a warm, sociable, steamy place redolent of cooking smells and passed-on cookbook spells. Here on the scrubbed wooden table are the sticky cakes, bowls of fragrant dried fruit and spices, nut roasts, strings of onions.

In spring come the soft-hued spheres of eggs, the rhubarb, the elderflowers, the marble-sized new potatoes, all waiting to be used with fresh young herb buds. Summer proffers salads, succulent soft fruits, iced lemonade with mint, delicate flower sorbets and herbal teas. Fall is the time for garnering in and storing our garden/hedgerow harvest: shining jars and bottles of chutneys, jellies, vinegars, and flavored oils; sweet burnished apples and huge pumpkins upon the shelf.

The myriad festivals and holidays that punctuate the seasons are encouragers of kinship as well as reminders of earth energies, mythologies, customs, and spiritualities past and present. They are rites of passage marking aspects of birth, sexuality, and death, ancient ways that modern people can appreciate and enjoy anew.

In the Southern Hemisphere the months when these seasons are enjoyed are different; the height of summer coincides with Christmas, and spring occurs when Europe and North America are getting ready for fall. The seasons can be celebrated in the traditional way just the same, substituting and/or incorporating local flora, myths, and legends as desired, and adapting the months to suit.

Spring is the time of regeneration and renewal, of victory of light over the forces of darkness. The sleeping Earth wakens, and the living world seems to stretch and expand itself. As the days start to warm up and grow longer, we start to spend more time out of doors.

A time of fertility, germination, and growth, spring is celebrated as Easter by Christians; as Purim (the Festival of Lots) by the Jews; as the Lantern Festival by the Chinese; and as Holi by Hindus. The Western word 'holiday' comes from Holi, festival of colors, and features bonfires, presents, and exuberant tossing of multicolored paint powder over friends and relatives.

In Ancient Greek mythology this was the time when Persephone, goddess of Spring, returned to meet her mother Ceres, the Corn goddess, after spending winter imprisoned underground by Pluto, the god of the underworld. In Ancient Rome Spring was marked by the festival of Flora, a vegetative deity, and everyone decked their doors and porches with garlands of flowering greenery.

May Festivals

The first of May in the Celtic calendar was called Beltane, when huge fires were lit on hilltops in honor of the sun god, and to herald summer's return. The plant of choice in Celtic Europe was usually 'may', or hawthorn, which gave protection against lightning, sorcery, ghosts, and malign fairies. Houses were spring-cleaned in honor of the festival, and hearths scrubbed to welcome the sacred 'need' fire, a brand of which was carried carefully from the Beltane blaze.

The Easter spring festival is of major importance in the Christian calendar – because it celebrates the resurrection of Jesus Christ– and the most significant for Greek orthodoxy. 'Easter' comes from 'Eostre', the Teutonic fertility goddess whose emblems were the egg and the hare – traditionally associated with the moon.

Egg Rituals

Easter Sunday celebrations often begin with breakfasting on painted, boiled eggs – the egg in many cultures being a symbol not only of birth but of the entire universe. Dyes used were usually made from plants, such as spinach, onions, and gorse. Eucalypt leaves make a range of subtle colors for contemporary egg-dyeing.

Hunting for eggs (whether painted or made of chocolate), hidden by the March Hare, is a most enjoyable Easter pastime. In the Jewish Pesach, or 'Passover', festival, which commemorates the Exodus of the Jews from Egypt, an egg is one of the special foods eaten at the *seder* ritual meal symbolizing the journey. 'Tongues of fire' are also the theme of the Christian festival of Whitsun, which is celebrated seven weeks after Easter Sunday. But this time the celebratory fire represents the descent of the holy spirit, wisdom, or 'wit', to the disciples of Jesus at the feast of Pentecost.

Many of the festive events during May, however, contain undercurrents of nature-veneration – maypoles (which represent the cosmic tree); parades of 'green men'; processions of virgins; and fertility dancing.

When the days reach their longest at the summer solstice, people all over Europe and Scandinavia traditionally give thanks for the bounteous luxuriance of nature. Midsummer's Eve and Midsummer Day at the end of June were times to celebrate the sun, a time of enchantment when faerie folk were said to leave their lairs to disport themselves among humans.

There was a break between haymaking and harvest, bonfires were lit, and while people cavorted eating lush fruit, gingerbread, and curd tarts they wore garlands of St John's wort, a solar flower, as a charm to keep away malign supernatural influences. People began to gather summer flowers and herbs for culinary use, beauty potions, and home physic – the herbs had to be plucked early in the morning with the dew still on them. Colonial New Englanders called herbs 'benefits' and dried them carefully out of the sun in the attic.

The Season of Love

Summer, being a time of visible fertility and cornucopia, has always been an auspicious time for weddings and hand-fastings. Midsummer magic was harnessed by those who wished to find out the identity of their true love; herbs and plants such as orpine were gathered and observed closely as a love oracle; if the plant inclined toward the left the beloved would eventually prove untrue.

In Europe certain holy wells with healing properties were 'dressed' with summer flowers, mud, and mosses before supplicants threw in coins and pins as gifts for the saint or water spirit. In Celtic tradition, water has always been a portal into other worlds. Summer is a time for questing after more spiritual desires – pilgrimages to holy places, sacred sites, and the magical geomantic patterns of mazes and labyrinths. Now is the time to make sacred journeys to Jerusalem, Mecca, Uluru (Ayers Rock), Stonehenge, and to the Hopi Kachina solstice dances in Arizona. Summer is also a time when fairs and fêtes, historical pageants and Independence Day parades abound under blue skies and puffy clouds.

Harvest Time

At the end of summer comes the ritual gathering of the harvest. To guarantee successful crop-garnering people invoke the gods as they have always done, from Demeter, the corn mother in Roman Europe, to the Maize Mother of Native Americans.

In the medieval Christian festival of Lammas, which was descended from Lugsanadh, the first cut corn of the harvest was presented to God in the form of a flat loaf. Lammas was also linked to the corn-dolly, a traditional fertility spirit fetish made from the last sheaf of uncut corn and fashioned into a braided favor. This harvest 'dolly' was kept in the farmer's kitchen to serve as a protection against illness and hunger.

In late summer Hindus celebrate Janmashtami, honoring the birth of Krishna when the new moon is first visible. Petals are scattered around each house, people wear floral garlands and images of the Krishna-child are placed in lavishly decorated small pavilions before a ceremonial feast begins.

*'People are going back and forth
Across the doorsill where the two worlds touch;
The door is round and open.
Do not go back to sleep.'*
Rumi, a Sufi poet

spring

s u m m e r

'How sweet I roam'd from field to field
And tasted all the summer's pride.
Till I the prince of love beheld
Who in the sunny beams did glide!

He shew'd me lilies for my hair,
And blushing roses for my brow;
He led me through his gardens fair,
Where all his golden pleasures grow.'

From 'Song', William Blake,
18th Century

fall

'Sing a song of Seasons!
Something bright in all!
Flowers in the summer,
Fires in the fall.'
From 'Autumn Fires' ,
Robert Louis Stevenson,
19th Century

winter

'That time of year thou mayst in me behold
When yellow leaves, or none, or few, do hang
Upon those boughs which shake against the cold,
Bare ruined choirs where late the sweet birds sang
In me thou see'st the twilight of such day ...'
Sonnet 73, Shakespeare

Fall is the time in northern climes when grass grows damp, leaves turn yellow and red, fruits are overripe, and like squirrels we store away foodstuffs for the anticipated long hard winter ahead.

The apple orchard has always been a sacred place – underlined in stories about the magic 'Apple Isle' of Avalon, and the dragon-guarded golden apples of the island of the Hesperides. Aphrodite and Eve are always pictured carrying apples, and the fruit features constantly in fairy tales. The Midwest's love of apples was promoted in the eighteenth century by a wandering preacher and plantsman who went by the name of Johnny Appleseed, who dispensed apple-tree seedlings to his congregations.

Giving Thanks

Now that the pantry was groaning with plenty, a generous fall was a time of many festivals. German households, for example, gave thanks not only in church and bierkeller but at home, where there was a designated 'God's Corner' – a mini-harvest festival heaped high with fruit and floral tributes, and a sample of the Frau's best baking and bottled preserves. For this was the time in rural communities everywhere when the huge gleaming copper preserving pans or giant pickling jars came into their own – bubbling with blackberries; or bright with ketchups and pickles. These days fresh fruit and vegetables are procurable all the year round from a worldwide larder, so home food preservation is not strictly necessary. But for many reasons – self-sufficiency, anxiety about pesticides, direct linking with nature, and, last but not least, taste – have a go at growing your own fruit and vegetables and preserving them.

The Origins of Hallowe'en

Samhain marked the beginning of the winter season of cold and austerity in countries with Celtic traditions. This 'new year' festival was also associated with death – decaying plants and flowers, and dwindling daylight. Samhain Eve became known as Hallowe'en – these days a night of ghoulish pranks, grinning pumpkin lanterns, and grotesque party food. Not so long ago it was believed to be a genuinely eerie 'in between worlds' night when fairies, witches, and goblins mixed with the living. The jack-o-lantern pumpkins and turnips would warn away ghouls and witches. Ritual games, such as bobbing or ducking for apples and love divination by nut-cracking, can still provide jovial entertainment. 'Trick or treating' probably comes from All Souls' Eve, when young children would go from house to house begging for small spiced buns known as 'soul cakes'.

Fall is the time for Rosh Hashanah, the Jewish New Year. This introspective time of soul-searching and augury is heralded by the blowing in the synagogue of the *shofar*, or ram's horn. In ancient days, ritual cleansing involved casting personal sins into a body of water before the Day of Atonement ten days later. For Hindus, the Diwali festival of light marks the end of the monsoon season and the beginning of Indian winter.

Rampant commercialism threatens to engulf the Christmas season altogether with its hollow razzmatazz, gift-buying frenzy, and instant party foods. It is restoring to the spirit then, at this time of year, to visit a well-used, well-lived-in kitchen that truly is the soul of the house. In the comforting fug of a real kitchen, battered beloved cookbooks are taken down and culinary alchemy enthusiastically undertaken to create festive dishes with a rich history and mythology.

Yuletide Customs

One of the loveliest Yuletide customs is the lighting of a candle each suppertime during Advent. Jewish people light candles now during Hanukkah, the Festival of Lights. Though the Christmas tree as we know it was popularized in England by Queen Victoria's consort Prince Albert, the concept of decorating a sacred tree is traditional in many cultures. You could decorate your living tree with nuts and special birdseed cake cut into star and moon shapes, so that when you plant it outside it is already wearing a winter present for the birds in your garden.

At the winter solstice in pre-Christian times people decked their houses with evergreen branches representing everlasting life and resurrection. At the annual Thanksgiving, Americans recall the early hardships and triumphs of the seventeenth-century New England colonists who managed to survive only by eating corn, the mainstay of the Algonquin diet. Thanksgiving garlands of greenery are festooned with honorary husks of corn as a visual memoir.

The festivities and rituals now associated with Christmas were, in the Celtic tradition, a thanksgiving to the gods for winter food supplies. They were also a supplication for the sun to return to grow the next year's crops.

Midwinter Gifts

The concept of giving presents in midwinter is not just a European one. The Pacific coast tribes of Native Americans have traditionally given each other generous midwinter gifts of food and canoes at their Potlatch feasts.

Named after Janus, the old Roman god of doorways who stares equally into history and futurity, January has always been associated with vows, luck-bringing activities, and fertility rites. A piece of coal, a coin, and a piece of bread are the traditional gifts of the 'dark haired man', who must be the first to step over the Scottish threshold at the stroke of midnight on New Year's Eve.

Twelfth Night is traditionally the last night that Christmas greenery and decorations can be kept up. Since classical antiquity, this has been a night of masks, forfeits, and merriment. Apple trees were 'wassailed' (sang to and offered a libation of cider) this month in the west of England.

Throughout Christian Europe people celebrate Epiphany, the visit of the Magi to Christ, and decorate homemade cribs with flowers. And in Southern India Hindus use floral decorations to celebrate Pongal, a harvest festival, when the sun enters Capricorn. The effigy of the sun-god Surya is garlanded in the household shrine with 'pongal'-cakes, sweet white rice, and rose water.

sensations

Our senses are subjective tools which enable us to interpret our environment and develop our individual esthetic view of it. After a while our senses begin to tell us what sensations – light and space, sounds and smells, colors and textures, aspects and objects – we will find most harmonious and pleasing in the home.

Often the design forms, textures, and resonances which we find most beautiful and uplifting come directly from, or are inspired by, the natural world. Organic shapes are innately pleasing, whether they be undulating stone window moldings or old rough-hewn floorboards.

A Sense of Belonging

Anchoring your home to its setting and your personality is an art that beckons the most eloquent colors and textures, that weaves light and space like a conjuror, and creatively juxtaposes the evocative powers of sound and aroma. The jigsaw pieces come together to shape a seamless sense of belonging.

For each of us 'spirit of place' and a home with 'soul' mean something different. For some with a monastic turn of mind it means stark, sparsely furnished rooms where the few decorative objects and artworks are exquisitely simple and have a meaningful esthetic and an important spatial relationship. For others it is a haphazard but romantically appealing hideaway that seems to sprout naturally from the landscape; a retreat where the inner batteries of the soul are re-charged and the Great Outdoors communed with.

Surprises for the Senses

Whatever Shangri-La we aspire to, whether super-modern or historic, country or town, it should delight our senses both physically and esthetically, and fuel our anticipation by constantly providing us with surprises. The only way it can do this is by relating to the changes in nature and heightening our awareness of the sensitivity of our five senses.

The changes we need to make to do this are not so great. By providing windows/skylights in the right spot, for example, we can let in bright sunlight and moonlight to transform a room from gloom to differing degrees of natural radiance. By planting a fruit tree outside a window we can enjoy the smell of spring blossom and the bright colors of fall berries. Windchimes can either lazily tinkle in a summer zephyr or make a melodic din as a storm approaches.

Making winding pathways outside to 'rewarding' idiosyncratic destinations, such as a shell-ringed pond, offers the opportunity to re-visit the tantalizing mysteries and dreamy sensory delights of childhood. Different times of day or night, different weather and seasons proffer a wealth of sensory variance to stimulate and challenge us anew.

For the senses are our only real passport to memory. Sensory experiences are, in fact, difficult to remember using the intellect. People, places, and events can be instantly evoked, memory re-awakened, by a taste or touch of this and a sniff of that. For example, the downy texture of an old velvet pillow might conjure yesteryear's party dress. Our senses are far more sensitive than we think, and sensory deprivation is a major cause of human disorientation. We need sensations: stimulating messages from the energies of the external world to thrive with physical, spiritual, emotional health.

Sensory Experiences

Truly memorable and intense sensory experiences stimulate all our senses at once and imprint themselves on our subconscious. Sitting by a pungently aromatic fire watching and listening to its crackling flames, experiencing the tactile warming of the cold iron poker in our hands, sipping mulled spiced wine – this is an all-embracing sensory scenario. The visual elements in a home are very certainly important, and so is aural stimulation and deep silence. Perhaps the most undervalued sensation faculties in our consciousness are those of touch and smell. The Shakers, who ordered their lives by the demands of the seasons and the beloved land they worked, were well aware of the healing qualities of these senses. Their master-crafted drawers were stacked with aromatic medicinal and household herbs, as well as tin canisters of the rich beeswax they used to maintain a satin sheen on their woodwork. The result was that all Shaker buildings had a memorable smell of beeswax and lavender, and every feature a smooth, tactile homeliness.

Ecological Soundness

Our homes are both a protection of, and an expressive sounding board for, self. Yet we should take great care that, whatever our symbology or decorative leanings, the actual fabric of our habitat is as ecologically sound as possible. We need not jeopardize our sensory need for sensation, though we may have to be more creative. Wherever possible use reclaimed or sustainable building materials of a non-artificial origin, local if possible; nontoxic paints; simple water and energy-conserving systems; and a naturally produced ambient indoor climate wherever possible.

So-called 'sick building syndrome', responsible for mass absenteeism in modern offices, has caused psychologists and architects to pioneer forward-thinking projects banning glaring overhead lighting, over-recycled air, and unopenable windows and create instead imaginative, softly lit work environments enlivened by plants and images.

light

'Then is his soul a lamp whose light is steady, for it burns in a shelter where no winds come.'
Bhagavad Gita

To be 'enlightened' means to be instructed or informed. It has also long been equated with spiritual uplift and divinity. Its importance in our vocabulary and in the theology of many civilizations cannot be overstated. Many belief systems are based on the premise that day and light represent life, while night and darkness are equated with death, and the dawn is a time of joyful resurrection.

All representatives of light are filled, therefore, with symbolism. The zigzag of lightning illuminating the dark sky is an emblem of shamanism; a link between our world and others. The candle is universally seen as a representative of individual consciousness of the human soul, a flame of knowledge and awareness of cosmic presence and power.

Without the radiation from the sun neither the human race nor any other living thing would have evolved. The universe is filled with light of varying grades and density. Light is the means by which our eyes see, receive, and we process information about our world. It gives our imaginings physical shape and heightens the intensity of all our senses.

Lack of Light

The amount of sunlight reaching into our homes affects not only our state of mind but our physical well-being, too. In the winter, millions of people suffer from SAD, or Seasonal Affective Disorder. Their hormones are affected by lack of daylight, causing depression, fatigue, and weight gain.

We need to optimize natural daylight and moonlight in our homes, supplemented by imaginative and sensitive artificial lighting. Our use of space can also affect the amount of light we enjoy. Space and light often go hand in hand. For example, tall windows swooping up to the ceiling invariably make a room look vast, airy, and flooded with fizzy bright light. Arabic countries, where

45

the light is glaring bright in the middle of the day, favor few windows in their houses. Small, secretive inner courtyards provide shaded illumination where people can work and rest in comfort. In more northern climes people want to maximize light in their homes. Parisian apartment blocks, for example, often have narrow central 'light wells' in the manner of giant skylights, which let in shafts of light to street level.

Add-on Structures

Some people get over the problem of admitting more light and space by building on extension-cum-conservatories. These add-on structures, first utilized by the Ancient Romans, have the advantage of being an excellent habitat for plants, thus connecting the house and garden in a boundary-blurred way. These glasshouses need not look suburban, and can incorporate up-to-the-minute soothing contemporary design features such as a waterfall dripping like rain down a feature window into a tropical pool. Light can be reflected back into the living area by using light-colored gravel or paving slabs just outside.

While knocking through from one living space to another, painting with off-white, and using pale-colored floorboards creates a wide-open vista that seems to flow naturally, sculpt space, and attract brightness, we must not forget that the human eye enjoys an atmospheric contrast of light and shadow. Such contrasts can be created by arcs of light from low-voltage lighting; hidden 'invisible' lighting in 'warm white' in poky corners and stairwells; peripheral uplighters silhouetting a special object;

pools of light and dark with small spotlights on a dimmer switch. These effects can be emphasized by the diffusing qualities of slatted shutters and gossamer-thin ethereal drapes; or colored glass in doors, screens, and lampshades which transform the light.

Mirrors represent divine truth and, to Taoists, the reflection of the universe; they are the 'soul-catchers' of the Ancient Egyptians and Celts. Their reflective surfaces are useful tricksters of light and space in narrow dark corridors. When fragmented, as in tiny mosaic mirror-tiles, they create a truly magical effect.

Mood-Creating Candles

Candles are, of course, the most mood-creative form of lighting, far more preferable to evenly spread artificial light for a social occasion. They can be used most effectively in a mirrored wall-sconce or massed on a mantelpiece in front of a gigantic overmantel mirror. Whether Spanish monastery tapers, English church candles, or the orange Buddhist sandalwood candle, they completely change the function of a room and add an air of mystique and meditation, especially when accompanied by incense. In terra-cotta pots or hurricane-lamps, nightlights scintillating in their dozens in dishes – whatever their shape, form, or radiance candles look fabulous.

'Architecture is always the spatial expression of a spiritual decision'
Ludwig Mies van der Rohe,
architect

s p a c e

Achieving a sense of space in your home is largely a matter of good lighting, which 'sculpts' an area into the shape you want. Designing with light is largely an illusionist's knack – and when you are fortunate enough to have either a new house built to your specifications or are redesigning/restoring an old dwelling, you can add new windows in imaginative positions. When the shafts of light from these brand new apertures merge into cross lighting from an existing window a remarkable sense of roominess and space is created.

Simplicity and Form

As the Shakers used to stunning effect, superbly simple craftsmanship married to pleasing form in uncluttered interior design are the great enablers when you want to create a sense of space and calm. You can achieve the latter by a disciplined weeding-out of objects and furnishings until only those things remain which you think are either intrinsically lovely, uniquely orna-

mental, or personally meaningful. As Utopian poet, artist, designer William Morris instructed his followers in 1882: 'Have nothing in your houses that you do not know to be useful, or believe to be beautiful'. This does not mean that Zen-like minimalism has to be adopted unless that is a lifestyle you particularly subscribe to. Near-empty rooms, especially in monolithic structures, often do have an ascetic, spiritual air alongside their feeling of volume and linear beauty.

Most of us, however, do not find such stringent simplicity easy, comfortable, or desirable. We prefer to compromise. We should certainly use the clean lines and sparse furnishings to lend a mysterious approach to our transitional spaces like halls and stairways, where our attention can concentrate both on the intrinsic character of the 'empty' space and our inner thoughts as we wander nomadlike, between living spaces.

Large expanses of surfaces in organic substances – granite, for example, or reclaimed wood – can also add both an interesting spatial dimension

47

and a direct relationship with nature. One should not subscribe, however, to the view of early twentieth-century Viennese architect Adolf Loos, who declared that 'ornament is crime'!

Clever storage is the secret weapon of the person who cannot bear to dispose of extraneous ephemera and eclectic household junk. If you are fortunate enough to have high ceilings, let your cupboards soar up the walls and utilize a stepladder. Just as in a tall, narrow room a clever balcony can double the usable space. So in a tall, narrow outside space cunning decking can instantly provide you with a bower/storage space, a 'magic staircase' and an elevated viewpoint for entertaining or skywatching.

As a room changes spatially with the application of, or removal of, color (pale, unusual, neutral colors are the best choice for a feeling of airy space), so furniture can be 'reinvented' by an ethereal lick of limewash, a swathe of draped plain calico, and a different position in the room or house. Perhaps the ornate but delapidated dining-room chair misfit can become an elegantly glacial gothic throne; the battered junk-store couch becomes a dreamy boudoir daybed.

Placement Disciplines

The composition and placement of objects is not only an art form in some cultures, it is part of their religious heritage and holistic life-view. Houses as well as household objects are subject to strict placement disciplines governed by earth energies. Native Americans usually like the doorways of their tipis or hogans to face either southwest or east, and inside every household object has its allotted place.

The Taoist Chinese practice of *feng shui* (meaning 'wind' and 'water') is an ancient geomantic divining discipline concerned with the relationship between human beings and two great energy fields: the consistent power of the Earth below us and the energy of the cosmos. The art of the *feng shui* expert is to understand these energies, and how they affect and influence the lives of individual people.

Feng shui (which has been labeled 'mystical interior design') is today used by many ordinary people in the East and West to modify and harmonize the siting of their dwellings, offices, and rooms, and to bring more balance and harmony to their lives.

Directing Good Energy

To obtain 'good energy' in their homes people try to arrange the interior so that the twin interactive, complementary forces of yin (dark, feminine) and yang (light, masculine) are in balance with their own personal energies. It is also necessary to take into account the auspicious and inauspicious energies of shape, form, and color.

There are no hard and fast rules to *feng shui*. Everything depends on how your energies correspond to those of your surroundings. So a water-stoop on the way to your front door may be fortuitous, but not necessarily! It is thought that mirrors positioned opposite windows produce disruptive energy and that working or sleeping directly opposite a doorway is not good for emotional or physical health. Soft, curved organic shapes may engender a positive flow of energy. Thus a display grouping of large rounded dark stones and creamy moonlike gargantuan candles should produce a feeling of euphoric well-being.

Feng shui practitioners do not much care for corridors that run straight from the front of the house to the back, as it is thought that this arrangement is not conducive to *ch'i* circulation. Sometimes a spirit screen (*ying pei*) is required to prevent the outward flow of beneficial energy or to shield the occupants of a room from negative energy.

In the Orient it is traditional to divide large internal spaces with screens to achieve the required room symmetry. In the West people are a little shy of using screens for some reason – but at the least they can lend a sense of theater to a room as well as hide unesthetic clutter.

'The music that I long to hear'
from 'The Habit of Perfection',
Gerard Manley Hopkins, 1866

s o u n d

The vibrational energy that is sound works on all our senses at once, at both a conscious and unconscious level. We only actually 'hear' a fraction of the sound energy around us; other members of the animal kingdom have a much more acute sensitivity to higher vibrations, as anyone who owns a cat or dog is aware. Family bustle, and the hum and buzz of office chat and machinery, can make us yearn occasionally for the healing calm of silence. Even the tranquility of the latter usually incorporates a considerable amount of sound, but it is probably the subliminal distant background noise of nature about her work and we do not think it unwelcome or intrusive. The ocean

sucking backward from the shore and then pounding back onto it is a primeval sound-pulse most of us feel energized and uplifted by, and wistfully yearn for in a childlike way every time we put our ears to a shell. Unless you actually live near the ocean, you will have to introduce soothing water sounds from a water feature within the house or just outside the window.

Buildings with sophisticated air-conditioning systems have windows that rarely open. This is not only bad for physical health but on an emotional and spiritual level the inhabitants of such a structure experience a sense of isolation; do not feel connected to the universal sacred soundtrack of rushing wind, rustling leaves, the crack of thunder. These things seem to be experienced at one remove, as if on video or celluloid. By keeping windows open – even a crack – in all seasons means you can bring natural sounds in to your home – birdsong, wind, snowfall, insects, or plant life such as reeds and bamboo which rustle and rasp atmospherically. A windchime hanging in a window (thought to attract positive energies in *feng shui*), or an Aeolian harp played by the wind produces melodic magic.

Home Music

Music as a form of home entertainment and component of religious ritual has been popular with human beings since the dawn of civilization. Early Egyptians played trumpets, cymbals, reed pipes, lyres, sistrum-rattles, bells, guitars, harps, and tambourines both for domestic pleasure and in honor of the goddess Hathor, the patron of music and dancing. Later, the Ancient Greeks made merry in their homes in the spirit of Pan, the festive Arcadian god.

The Tibetan singing bowl – a metal bowl played by gently massaging the rim with a stick until it resonates – was an essential spiritual healing tool of the people of Tibet and Ladakh. It is now possible to buy modern custom-built bowls made of pure quartz crystal, tuned to the tone of the originals.

Other traditional ethnic instruments currently enjoying popularity for playing at home as well as in public include Tibetan gongs, tribal frame drums from Taos, New Mexico, and African djembe drums; the Irish bodhran drum, uillean pipes and flute; the Native American 'men's society' rattle; and a variety of North African percussive instruments. There has also been an upsurge of interest in 'breath work', which helps us concentrate on the intuitive rhythms of our breathing during the 'silence' of meditative states. Breathing is the link between our bodies and our conscious/unconscious minds. Simple exercises that focus totally on the life-sustaining process of inhalation and exhalation conjure 'stillness' through these sighing sounds of awareness. Classical music in the East always makes use of stillness between notes and tonal spacing to encourage contemplation – in the West the Gregorian chant is constructed in this way for the same reason.

Avoiding Noise Pollution

The negative aspect of sound that we all have to address in order to enjoy a peaceful home life is the ever-increasing problem of noise pollution. To achieve the degree of peace and well-being we require at home we have to shut out unwanted noise. In the garden, noise from neighbors and/or nearby traffic can be lessened by a dense planting of shrubs, preferably on a high earth bank. Inside, if you choose bare floorboards, flagstones, or quarry tiles, sound will echo more.

In apartments, noise from neighbors can be softened or blocked by thick, sound-absorbent cloth wall-hangings and heavy drapes. Walking barefoot indoors (and encouraging visitors to do the same) is both good for your feet, for your ears, and for the flooring.

smell

We have always known that aromas directly affect the way we feel both emotionally and physically. The olfactory nerves in our noses transmit unpleasant or pleasant odiferous information to our brains immediately, and we record this aromatic knowledge in our memories. Thus the remarkable powers of evocation of this sensory organ: a waft from baking bread or the scent of flowers drifting through an open window can transport us as if by magic to other places, other times, people, and events consigned to history. The haunting powers of smell have been used in the form of incense in mystical, religious ceremonies since ancient times in many cultures.

Revered Perfume

When in medieval times Arab traders (and the Crusaders) exported aromatic petals, barks, roots, resins, and gums to Europe the response was avid. At a time when disease and household stench was endemic, people felt perfume to be both medicinal and spiritually elevating. Strongly scented herbs such as rosemary, hyssop, and lavender, and flowers such as the rose were much utilized and regarded with reverence.

Medieval monasteries distilled floral waters, and everyday households took to mixing sweet-smelling 'strewing herbs' with the meadow hay and grasses they used as floor-covering. By the seventeenth century most housewives were skilled home apothecaries as well as cosmeticians, perfumers, and distillers of scented household products. Their spidery hand-written recipe books reveal knowledge and insight being used by aromatherapists today.

Aromatic lore was taken to America and Australia by the first settlers, who used it extensively both for practical reasons and to remind them of 'home'. In New England stalwart housewives made pomanders and sprinkled 'sweet waters' on their floors and linen. They quickly acclimatized themselves to native species of their favorite plants to supplement the seeds they had taken with them.

Violets, sacred to the Greek nymph Io, and farther elevated by the Christian church as having 'the odor of sanctity', were a popular indigenous ingredient, along with imported, naturalized cotton lavender and rue – 'the herb of grace' – to scent linen. The big brown seeds of naturalized sweet cicely (*Myrrhis odorata*) were rubbed on oak floorboards and furniture to impart gloss and a faint sweet odor. Special materials and treasured mementoes were kept in storage chests of cedar or hickory to preserve the contents – a custom well worth reviving today.

It was not long before the canny housewives borrowed from the extensive and complex aromatic medicine chests of Native Americans and Australians. The former adopted into their physic gardens Joe Pye Weed, used by the Iroquois as a fragrant tea for nerves and fevers; while Aboriginal lore about the many uses of the eucalypt was quickly absorbed into Australian daily life.

Natural Fragrances

A scented garden will allow you fully to enjoy the delicacy and subtlety of nature's gifts of fragrance and constantly fill your home with characterful displays of swooningly perfumed cut flowers. Even a balcony, windowbox, or hanging basket can still be useful and effective. The possible shrub/plant list is enormous and very personal. Mine would definitely include tobacco plants, daphnes, the Madonna lily, narcissi, Mexican orange, wisteria, bluebells, stocks, night-scented jasmine (only to be grown as a conservatory plant in northern Europe), mimosa, mock orange, and honeysuckle … plus herbs like lavender, sage, thyme, woodruff, lemon balm, bergamot, rosemary, basil, marjoram, and camomile. However wild or constrained your garden is, have a seat in it so you can languish in intoxicating perfumed shade.

Expressing Yourself

P erfuming with a rich array of odors is an expression of yourself. Choose spices from cloves, cassia, citrus peel, coriander, allspice, nutmeg, or cinnamon. For furniture polish, use quality beeswax, melt it in a double boiler and, after removing it from the flame, add a few drops of lavender oil. Scented candles can be made in a similar way, with, of course, the addition of a wick.

Vaporizing is another way of fragrancing our homes with delightful smells. Vaporizers are affordable ceramic containers which hold water and an essential oil. Heated by a nightlight underneath, they are effective and have a 'votive' look; they also add beneficial moisture to the air if you live in a house with a dry atmosphere. Spray-bottle plant-misters can be filled with water fragranced with a few drops of the appropriate oil – sensuous ylang ylang for the bedroom; uplifting, inspirational bergamot for the study; relaxing sandalwood for a gathering in the living room.

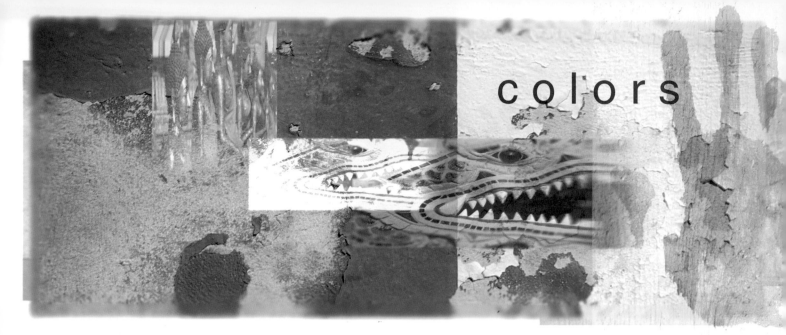

Our whole being, our physical, spiritual, and emotional body, is profoundly affected by color. Contained in the spectrum of light visible to humans, color is captured by the photoreceptors in our eyes and transmitted to our brains in the form of electrical impulses. It seems that the vibrations of some long wavelength colors such as red really can stimulate and energize us, while others, such as blue, at the other end of the spectrum, are cooling and relaxing.

Color Therapy

Though considerable contemporary research is under way into the healing power of colors, color therapy was used by the Ancient Egyptians, Greeks, and Romans. For the Greeks color was personified by the goddess Iris whose pathway between the divine and human was her seven-hued rainbow, beyond which was Seventh Heaven – Mount Olympus.

The spectacular-colored arcs of the rainbow have been of major significance in many mythologies for their metaphorical joining of heaven and Earth. In the Norse Edda sagas the rainbow was a bridge called Bifrost between the gods' home Asgard and Earth; while to the Bantu African peoples, Native North Americans and Australian Aboriginal tribes, the rainbow is an omnipotent cosmic snake arched across the sky.

Color Choices

Choosing colors for a room should ideally be an extremely personal decision, but alas in real-life situations compromise usually rears its head. But there are plenty of colors to choose from and an astonishingly wide range of stains, tints, and glazes can provide a room with a translucent whisper of color. Pure color pigment is available from dealers in nonchemical paint products for those who want to experiment with blocks of vivid color or color mixing, and specialist brushes, sponges, and combs can be bought at many hardware and do-it-yourself stores so that interesting textured finishes can be created on the paint surface itself before it dries.

Color for Self-Expression

The old-fashioned concept of neat polite color coordination was never any good for self-expression. The humanized version of color harmony looks at the many traditions, therapies, and mythologies associated with the color palette and reacts to them viscerally and emotionally to choose which suits our personal needs and creeds. A thoughtful and imaginative use of intense color can positively benefit our health by reminding us of warm, exotic places. The evocative powers of vivid indigo, Tuscan terra cotta, cobalt, aquamarine, sky blue, and jade green can transport us from a dreary winter's day to a far-flung foreign clime.

Color can be layered, the top tint gently rubbed off here and there to reveal hints of another 'secret' hue hidden beneath. Color can also be painted palely on floorboards to conjure a Scandinavian meeting-house, or in a riot of childlike polychromatic pattern around the frames of the windows and doors as people do to the façades of their houses in the bleakly beautiful southern deserts of Yemen and Saudi Arabia.

Added Texture

Just as contrasting collisions in color can be stimulating (for example, pale orange, cerise, pale green, and pale yellow), so can surprising texture mixtures. Checks, stripes, and florals can work well together, so can natural 'homespun' throws and richly embroidered, tapestry, or ethnic kelim carpet pillows. 'Touchy-feely' baroque-style embossed velvet, polished cotton, organza, and silk tafetta pillows and bolsters create an exotic atmosphere sited on stone window seats, austere wooden sofas, or anarchic metal garden thrones.

For a totally natural look, smell, and feel to a room, leave its pale brown-pink plaster finish unpainted, and just brushed with a clear glaze. If you have slabbed stone or hardwood timber floors, all the better, otherwise use floor-coverings made of seagrass, coir, or jute. Continue the basic, pared-down approach with calico or hessian curtains, handmade willow storage baskets, and honest rough-hewn locally crafted wooden furniture. Tall dried grasses and bulrushes in an unglazed pot or urn, and artlessly heaped fircones in the rustic open fireplace, would add the final touch to a charming simple scenario.

Many old vegetable-dyed tribal rugs from Morocco, India, Afghanistan, Iran, Arabia, and Tibet not only look wondrous; their faded patterns and colors are symbolic representations of myth, legend, and religious belief. Similarly, displaying themed meaningful pictures and decorative objects from many contrasting cultures can provide a feast of tactile and visual sensuality, of spiritual and creative stimulation. Groups of found objects of themed color and texture – a bowl of feathers, twigs, and egg-shaped stones and smooth opaque sea-glass, for example – can create a seasonally changing series of fantasy tableaux.

Using Color

The traditional spiritual/psychological associations of particular colors in the color wheel are worth experimenting with. Bear in mind that there are three systems to choose from. The monochromatic approach just uses one color in a variety of shades, while harmonious schemes use colors near each other on the color wheel, such as blue and green. Choosing contrasting colors which complement each other, meanwhile, can be challenging and satisfying. Remember, when choosing paints, that light colors make surfaces appear to recede, while warm shades bring them closer.

Yellow for Enlightenment
Intellectual color representing enlightenment and, in Islam, wisdom. Often used to express optimism and freedom, this vivid color, representative of the sun, is popular for home-offices and kitchens, where it promotes communication. Works well with shades of green in dining rooms and kitchens. Striking with brilliant white.

Red for Luck
Represents self-confidence, energy, invigoration, sexual power, and fire. Associated with blood, danger, and both the devil and the Christian church. In China and India it is a very lucky color. Reduces a sense of space and can make a room cozy – but if too bright it can be oppressive. Not restful for bedrooms, but can be revitalizing in work- and living rooms. Pale reds and pinks can be comforting and look wonderful against old wood. Looks opulent teamed with gold and turquoise.

Orange for Sacredness
Sacred, healthy, happy color in China and Japan. Buddhist monks wear saffron to denote joy in humility. Welcoming in hallways if in pastel form. Harmonizes well with blue, violet, and indigo.

Green for Harmony
Linked to nature, life, peace, and healing, green is an anxiety-lifting color chosen by ecology-minded people to denote the spirit of Gaia, Mother Earth. This hue of harmony and balance is in the middle of the spectrum.

Blue for Inspiration

Traditionally conjures reflective calm and spiritual inspiration. Associated with the heavens, often chosen for church and temple domes. The headdress worn by the Wandjina spirit ancestors painted on cave walls by Aboriginal Australians is always bright blue. A favored color, both in deep and pale, for bedrooms or meditation areas.

Indigo for Intuition

Used since ancient times to represent intuition, dreams, and the sacred. Popular in the Middle East to paint protective 'magic' lines around windows and doors. Spectacular with other colors for dramatic contrast and emphasis.

Violet for Royalty

Sometimes known as purple, violet has been associated with royalty since ancient times, when the dye was pricey. Also linked with intuition, artistic endeavor, psychic communication, and noble ideals, pale shades of violet are thought helpful for deep thought. Suitable therefore for meditation rooms, art/craft studios, and creative writing retreats. Teamed with dusty, ethereal tints of pink and blue it can turn a bedroom into a mystical haven.

White for Purity

Associated with purity and perfection, white can look spectacular in a simple room, historic or modern. Particularly effective in the warm neutral off-white provided by old-fashioned distemper, chalk-based paint or organic emulsion, especially when offset by natural materials. White is also useful to make a room look larger or a ceiling higher.

PART 2

Functions
for the
Home

Functions for the Home

Functions for the Home brings the knowledge acquired in Part One into the home and its immediate surroundings and suggests ways in which it can be used. The main focus of Chapter Four, Share & Sustain, is food and nurturing, in the broadest possible sense. Food and the sharing of it is a tactile, taste-bud titillating, way to enjoy the health-giving produce of nature, and an important role-player in folklore and religions around the world. We look at the kitchen as the home's energy center, as well as many methods of food gathering, conserving, storing, displaying, preparing, cooking, presenting, eating, and celebrating. Chapter Five, Be & Do, is an important, highly practical chapter which deals with the way we actually behave in our homes; our hobbies and activities, and how the way the home's boundaries and divisions affect each family member's privacy and communal conviviality alike. The emphasis here is on capturing the elusive spirit of place and time and boosting self-esteem by making new things, recycling old things, and indulging in creative, 'magical' gardening.

In Chapter Six, Cleanse, we discuss ritual purification and historical and contemporary cleansing methods for the body, household things, and clothing. Chapter Seven, Rejuvenate, gives restorative remedies and renewals of many kinds for both body and spirit in all parts of the house, but mainly bedrooms.

share & sustain

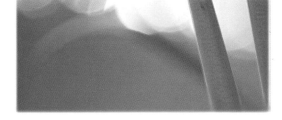

The image that the title of this chapter conjures immediately is that of nourishment and sustenance based on food preparation and dining rituals. Eating and drinking together is a powerful and positive social 'cement' for families and friendship. What keeps body and soul together is a mixture of the calorific and sensual value of the food itself plus small meaningful age-old ceremonies such as lighting candles and helping others to choice morsels.

In the modern world, of course, the complexity and chaos involved in juggling paid work, homecare, family duties, and leisure activities often mean that mealtimes are snatched snack affairs. But for physical and mental health we should sit down and give even that humble sandwich proper attention. Taking fifteen minutes out to eat properly from a plate – fresh foods rather than additive-laden convenience products – and perhaps have a relaxed chat with partner or child, will pay us back a hundredfold in terms of good digestion and lowered stress levels.

Optimal health, after all, is an achievable goal if we monitor what we eat and how we eat it. However, people's hunger and thirst is not just for things edible, and we should be aware in our home of the need to sensitively and with kindness sustain family and friends in their quest for spiritual and emotional fulfilment and self-understanding. It is perfectly normal for even those whose appetite for life is gargantuan to sometimes have feelings of inexplicable sadness and self-doubt. Wellness and a sense of well-being can often manifest itself after a bout of 'being out of sorts', when a problem has been shared with someone who has listened patiently and intently without judging or offering unlooked-for advice.

The transformational power of being a good listener, instinctive or self-trained, should never be underestimated, and is worth a cartload of hypertension medication. By the same token, in your home don't let the emotional blockage of heavy silence loiter about for days rather than discuss an important but difficult issue. Constructive conversation can be as healing for the heart and mind as good food is for the body. Any form of nurturing is a creative act which will give your home a warm atmosphere of goodwill and generosity.

Sustenance, then, can be of many sorts. Don't forget, when you are making the grocery list, the needs of your emotions, intellect, and spirit. Put on it a visit to the flower stall, and a side-trip to that comforting street with the twinkling windows and twisty fairytale steps.

Food has always played a central, complex role in human society, going far beyond its basic function of providing us with essential life-giving energy. Most cultures worship their deities with some sort of thanksgiving food-offering, real or symbolic. Food-gathering and sharing provide communal cohesion in many small social groups; and the universal traditions and rituals of hospitality revolve around the giving and receiving of food and drink.

Alas, here in the Western world, factors such as the large-scale take-over of farming by high-tech agri-business, the proliferation of bland, giant food superstores, and the diaspora of families, have combined in the recent past to crush our deep-seated reverence for food and its folklore.

Wholesome Alternatives

Happily there is a growing backlash band of committed organic farmers, backyard deep ecologists, and kitchen-table bottlers, picklers, and pie-makers who are offering wholesome alternatives to chemically sprayed fruit and vegetables and forgettable mass-produced instant 'meals'. With this rediscovery of old sustainable agricultural practices, healthy traditional whole foods from around the world and the pleasure of interpreting traditional multicultural food preparation and dining rituals comes an awareness of the issues of world hunger, Western obesity and food waste, and the obscenity of the food mountains stored by wealthy countries.

Part of the new personal responsibility for providing nutritious, additive, and pesticide-free food for family and friends and keeping a stringent eye on what goes in the garbage can (all homes should have a special bin for recycling vegetable waste for garden compost), is a rediscovered reverence of the 'sacredness' of our basic life-giving foods.

The Staff of Life

Bread was certainly a holy food for the Ancient Egyptians, whose chief deity, Osiris, was also known as the God of Grain. Workers on the great pyramid of Cheops were paid in flat loaves. For the early Celts any form of grain was a gift from the Corn Mother, and the bread they made was not only food but cult fertility object and good luck amulet (new babies had bread put in their cradles or tied to their clothes to protect them against the evil eye). The 'magic' of rising bread is meant to be enhanced by the right-handed stirring of the dough mixture 'sunwise'. For the Incas and Aztecs, crescent-moon-shaped quinoa grains and vivid sky-blue cornmeal (later much utilized by Hopi Native Americans), were not only the ingredients of the favored breads of the people but were thought to be the sacred, mystic grain eaten by the sky gods.

Those early battlers against the adulteration of bread, the Shakers, venerated the 'live germ' within the homegrown grain they used to make their flour, and made their wide variety of loaves in bare, clean kitchens of almost holy simplicity. The ever-practical piety of the Shaker 'kitchen sisters' would have approved of English poet John

Masefield's poem, which underlines the spiritual link between corn and the bread made from it, 'by which the soul of man is fed'.

The Humble Apple

Many of the fruit and vegetables we eat have fascinating growing histories and mythologies, perhaps none more so than the humble apple. Related to the rose family, apples are symbols of both Aphrodite and Eve, and represent immortality, thus their appearance in many European fairytales.

For gypsies all over the world the apple is sacred because of the mysterious five-pointed 'pentacle' shape at its core when it is cut in half. Celtic tradition held that the legendary paradisical island of Avalon, ruled by magic herbalist Morgan and nine holy sisters, was covered by an orchard of apple trees, one of which was the Tree of Life.

Sensible Food Storage

A well-stocked pantry, the survival safety-net of the colonial housewife and her European ancestors, was a practical place of great atmosphere and romantic beauty. If you have the room, this is a food-storage place to emulate, for the storage systems of antiquity were in fact very sensible. The huge marble or stone slabs were piled high with still-life vignettes: great sculptural chunks of cheese lurked under cheesecloth shrouds, bread peeped out of earthenware crocks, vegetables brimmed from tubs of sand, and eggs and apples nestled in straw. Jars and bottles of

The areas of food preparation, such as this humble marble sink outside a Tuscan house, are sites not only of holistic healthy bodily sustenance but also of folk nostalgia for yesteryear's symbolic, mythic importance of food. These are the places where that all-important sensory attribute taste rules in its own very sensual kingdom.

multicolored seasonal preserves, scented vinegars, and unusual-flavored oils gleamed from behind great festooned ropes of onions and garlic (revered by the Ancient Egyptians as symbols of immortality and physical strength), while on other shelves rough sacks of grains and flour stood in readiness for baking. Over everything hung the sweet savor of the mystic-East-evocative spices, kept locked in labeled wooden apothecary-style drawers, mingled with the perfumes of the herb bundles hanging from the rafters.

Reap and Sow

To enable us to recapture a little of the old country calendar of sowing, reaping, and storing we must make a kitchen garden plot (this can be in an old sink or a few giant flowerpots if you are a city-dwelling urban farmer with only a windowsill, rooftop eyrie, or balcony). Vegetable and fruit garden-making, even on a tiny scale, can be an important learning tool for children, who these days may be aware of food only as a product chosen from supermarket shelves. A particularly interesting project for little ones is to grow a small tree or bush from a pip or seed they were about to throw into the garbage, and to regularly feed it when it germinates from the compost heap they helped make from kitchen waste.

When the children visit the ocean get them to collect some seaweed to feed their plant, along with some shells to decorate it. Watering the kitchen garden can also be an exercise in recycling, with the help of the vegetable-rinsing water, dish water, and tea leaves. Remind yourself and your children of the crisp delights to come if the plants are conscientiously looked after, by making a varnished découpage sink splashback out of bright seed-packages. Harvesting the fruits of edible plants you have grown from seed, such as zucchini, eggplant, and tomato can be most satisfying, especially if you can keep back some from the stove to save in the pantry for a winter's day. Opening a homemade edible timecapsule such as this and savoring the distinctive scents and flavors of spring, summer, or fall is, indeed, a sublimely celebratory moment.

The Edible Garden

You don't have to be particularly green-thumbed to successfully grow a very productive herb and edible-flower garden. Having these fresh means not only interesting, unusual salads and garnishes but also flowers to crystallize and herbs to hang up and dry (somewhere shady) for culinary or tea/tisane purposes, to use in decorative sprigs, to add subtle flavor to oils, vinegars, home-made cordials, or bottled fruit in syrup. Honey, reminiscent of the cosmic golden nectar that made the gods immortal on Mount Olympus, and heir to a vast amount of sacred-bee mythology, can also be flavored for the home pantry with vanilla beans, ginger, and homegrown herbs. Lavender, the darker the color the better,

An atmospheric venue for kitchen alchemies. Marcel Proust described just such a place in *À La Recherche du Temps Perdu*: 'The back kitchen seemed not so much the cave of Françoise as a little temple of Venus. It would be overflowing with the offerings of the dairyman, the fruiterer, the greengrocer, come sometimes from distant villages to dedicate to the goddess the first fruits of the fields.'

The atmosphere of the kitchen itself is of vital importance, as usually family and visitors naturally gravitate there while the host/hostess is cooking, and often in an apartment it is the only venue for dining. A paint backdrop of sunflower-yellow and pistachio green suggests *joie de vivre*.

will add a smoky mystique to a jar of runny honey. Use about three small fresh flower heads for an average jar, stir in well and leave for about a week before using. Not to be utilized, though, for those who seek amorous success, for lavender has in the past been used extensively in charms and concoctions to preserve chastity!

Storing Herbs

You must remember to store your herbs as soon as they are dried, for in humid weather they may go moldy. People usually take the leaves from the stem (except those kept back for *bouquet garni* bundles), before putting them in a clean, airtight jar, glass, or earthenware pot, in a dark corner of the pantry. Marigold petals can be stored this way also, but other flowers should be kept in bunches in labeled paper bags.

Remember that crumbled leaves and flowers used for cooking are less aromatic than those used whole. A very effective way of storing pretty summer herb leaves and flowers such as borage is to freeze them in the water-filled compartments of an ice cake; these iced florals add a touch of ethereal magic to any cocktail party.

Flowers can also be preserved for cake decoration. For something different use the tubular scarlet blossoms of bergamot or lemon balm, beloved by butterflies, as well as popular with Native Americans for Oswego tea. Some flower-preservation methods use gum arabic, but the simplest way with tiny flowers like violets is to paint them lightly with beaten egg-white using a fine artists' brush, dust them with confectioners' or superfine sugar, and, most important, store them in an efficiently airtight container.

Preserves and Pickles

Kitchen spices, those aromatic ambassadors of faraway places, bring the flavors of the world to our dinner tables, and deserve to be kept respectfully. King Solomon received gold, jewels, and spices from the Queen of Sheba, so it's the least we can do to store these high-ranking condiments in airtight containers, away from the stove and cooking smells, in a cool, dark place like the pantry or cupboard. Experimenting with spices is an almost alchemical experience … a little pinch of this red powder or those black grains and we are conjured as if by magic carpet to sultry Sri Lanka or the icy northern tracts of Scandinavia.

Jam and jelly-making is a mouthwatering, fun activity for family and friends to enjoy, especially

Use reclaimed tiles from your local salvage yard as a patchwork splashback behind the sink, sometimes a mismatched assortment with a similar color scheme is quirkily effective. This green and pink tiling scheme (overleaf) comes from an *arrière-cuisine* in a house in Salernes, South of France.

if the preserving-pan session is preceded by a berry-gathering picnic or an *en-masse* trip to the farm-stand or local farmers' market for figs, quinces, apricots, apples, or redcurrants. Experiment by adding a few herbs to the mixture: infuse your batches with rosemary, thyme, mint, or sage to add verve to a winter roast later in the year.

If you make a mistake with your recipe and it sets a little hard, cut your stiff jam into squares and serve it as an English seventeeth-century 'fruit cheese' confectionery conceit called Quiddony; or tell your guests you have made fruitcake in the traditional Canadian Chippewa way!

As with all kinds of pickle, preserve-making, and home-bottling it adds to the quaint charm of the pantry and later presentation on the table if the containers used are pretty and/or unusual. It's worth recycling nice bath-oil or bath-salts bottles and jars (well-washed out) for this purpose, as well as glass mineral water bottles in luminous lavender-blue and soft sea-green.

Home-spiced oils (chili, basil, or mustard-seed), and vinegars (roses, nasturtiums, chive, shallot, or strawberry), look very exotic in containers like these, and it's fascinating researching the symbolism of your chosen ingredients.

Vinaigre Rouge

Here, for example, is a very simple old French vinegar recipe, called Vinaigre Rouge 'St Laurent' from the Pyrenees. Of exceptional flavor and fragrance, it uses the deep-red petals of the rose, emblem of divine love,

heavenly bliss, and confessional secrecy: Heat two cups of good white vinegar in a nonaluminum saucepan. Do not allow to boil. Meanwhile, put half a cup of dark-red rose petals in a jar with a non-metal lid. Pour your hot vinegar over the petals, leaving about half an inch to spare at the top. Cool your infusion at room temperature, and allow to sit for about a month, covered. Strain and pour into an attractive bottle, adding a fresh red rosebud before sealing.

Grain Storage

Ceres, the great European mother goddess of the grain harvest, has presided over all edible seeds and grains since Ancient Roman times, as the Corn Maiden has done for many Native American tribes. All civilizations have milled grain to make flour and some sort of bread, and all have agonized about the best way to store it free from damp and animal or insect predation. Traditionally, Native Americans store their corn by suspending it from the ceiling of the tipi or hogan, while some African peoples keep their cereals in granary storerooms which can only be entered by a hole in the ceiling. Nomadic Australian Aboriginal women transport desert grass seed for making damper bread around with

Make a virtue of necessity. You need to keep your kitchen implements and condiments conveniently to hand, so an attractive display of carefully graded gleaming pans brings order to a varied collection of kitchen accoutrements.

them in their portable 'dilly-bag' pantries made of woven pandanus leaves.

Staples Storage

Good storage of staples such as wheat, rye, corn, oats, millet, barley, and rice (watched over in Balinese granaries by Dewi Sri, the rice goddess), has always been most important, for without it the powerhouse of minerals locked within the grains is spoiled and lost. One of the most important food and medicine seeds to the Ancient Egyptians and the Cherokee Native Americans was the flaxseed, sacred to Isis and the sun gods … it is now popular as a salad component and an alternative medicine therapy for a large number of disorders.

The well-known nineteenth-century American household compendium *The Woman's Exchange Cook Book*, by Mrs Minnie Palmer, Chicago, firmly instructs her loyal readers that flour must not be kept anywhere damp, and, vitally, needs to be stored in an airtight container, for 'it readily absorbs odors that are perceptible to the sense'.

Pest Deterrents

A dry, cool, dark-ish old-fashioned pantry, surrounded by a harvest festival of edible goods, is the perfect setting for the noble grain. Simple pest-deterrents used way back in Elizabethan times still work perfectly well today: mice can be prevented from ever entering the pantry by a scattering of aniseed and mint, while big lazy bluebottles and blowflies veer sharply away from hanging bunches of dried nettles, rue, and bitter, aromatic tansy – one of many herbs dedicated to the Virgin Mary.

Rediscovered Grains

Some rediscovered 'gourmet' grains such as amaranth were once used in religious ceremonies by peoples as diverse as the Aztecs, the Ancient Greeks, and medieval Christians, who used its purple, pink, gold, and red seed-heads as symbols of eternity and immortality.

In this day and age the grain-pantry can be truly international – one can buy in health-food stores, for example, Russian buckwheat, Indian rice, Mexican corn, Scottish oats, Ethiopian teff, Afghani barley, and Egyptian spelt, made as in the days of the Pharaohs, from the dried sacred lotus.

When buying grains, or fresh fruit and vegetables, it is important to make sure they are the very best of what the combination of land, air, and water have to offer.

For other natural products, investigate small, delicious-smelling specialist ethnic stores where the interesting smells of garlic, olives, cheeses, nuts, and seeds stimulate your taste buds and get your appetite and imagination really going.

A Feast on the Shelf

A global village theme on the pantry shelves can provide a multicolored visual feast, a veritable kitchen bazaar or souk. Don't hide your packaging away. Juxtapose distinctively colored or designed packages, jars, and cans to create your own art form: here Chinese canned lychees, there a box of pastel-wrapped Italian amaretto cookies … farther along English mustard, French cassis cordial, Latin American panela sugar loaf, Indian rosewater, Israeli matzos, Colombian coffee, Tunisian chili paste, and a jar of Japanese mushrooms. This surely is the place to light a small votive candle of grateful thanks to the Hindu goddess of food and bounty, Anapurna.

The Art of Cooking

When one thinks of all the sensations, moods, and memories conjured up by mealtimes, one realizes how monumentally important the art of cooking is. By this I do not mean that every act of eating has to be an epicurean triumph, but that ingredients should always be fresh, appealing, and in season, and the preparation of the food an enjoyable creative ritual. Subtle nuances of color, flavor, and texture can be most effective with the simplest of economical, uncooked summery peasant dishes – think of a humble chunk of fresh homebaked bread, a big, sweet, juicy homegrown tomato in a pond of limpid pale-green virgin olive oil, with a small pyramid of crumbly sea salt on the side.

The Joys of Preparation

Preparing and cooking food has always been a far from dull occupation, for not only is there the sensual pleasure of the food itself, there is the ritual and mythology in preparation and the alchemy of the seasoning process. In

A sumptuous display of fresh, locally grown, vegetables and produce, or as Proust called them: 'exquisite creatures who had been pleased to assume vegetable form', lures us into the kitchen.

ancient times the hearth – the house's heart and 'altar' – was also the place where the cooking took place, adding a spiritual dimension to culinary art. Our choice of food ingredients and the way we prepare them reflect our sense of place, our feeling for history, and our cultural identity. Small wonder then that with so many people now searching for their roots, 'heritage' recipes of various kinds are very popular. While stirring the pot or kneading

the dough the cook can enjoy a time-warp escapist reverie and be transported in his or her imagination to a very different sort of kitchen.

Festival Cooking Rituals

Many of the year's festivals come with cooking rituals attached. When we make a Christmas plum pudding, for example, we are taking part in a pagan ritual, for our rich, fruit-stuffed dessert began life in Celtic times as a milky cornmeal gruel, stirred sunwise, and served to guests at the solstice as an edible symbol of the god of plenty, Dagda. Many people still stir their puddings sunwise (clockwise) for luck without realizing the antiquity of this folk memory. Traditionally every member of the family has to stir the pudding for the luck to last all year. The holly which decks the pudding originally had another role – it was a sacred druid protective plant to shield the householders from evil spirits. Making mince pies is another venerable midwinter activity. If you want to make them the medieval way, you should make them oblong, heavily spiced, with meat and fruit inside and a pastry Christ child on top. If you enjoy baking (or live near an excellent bakery or deli) it is enjoyable and educational for children to taste Christmas food from other countries: German stollen cake; Dutch speculaas figurine cookies; Italian torrone; St Lucia's gingerbread from Sweden; sweet French fougasse bread … and so on.

Bread Lore

The Romans introduced bread-making ovens to other Europeans, who embraced this 'new technology' fervently. As Europe and North America seem to be currently enjoying a home-baking boom, it is interesting to note many of the bread-making traditions and taboos which have filtered down from ancient times. Indeed until this century in many Christian countries it would have been unthinkable for a sign of the cross to be made in the bread before it was set to rise, to protect the household from witchcraft and the devil. Loaves made on Christmas morning and Good Friday were believed to have especially magical properties; they were ground into a powder and put into the first-aid kit. Many homes had a cross made of rowan tied with red thread (an old anti-supernatural device), nailed over the oven to protect the food from malign influence during the cooking process.

Spiced breads, a wonderful treat for breakfast or teatime, were popular in 1623, when John Murrell, in his recipe book, *A Delightfull Daily Exercise For Ladies and Gentlewomen*, suggested baking using ginger, nutmeg, a grain of musk and 'a thimble-full of the powder of an Oring-peele'. However, despite this exoticism, a contemporary book of etiquette still had to warn readers not to 'butter bread with your thumb'! Much of the old

Inventive table-setting using mellow candlelight and fall leaves adds autumnal atmosphere to this festive spread.

77

English baking lore went over to America, along with the recipes, with the first colonists.

It was not long, though, before the New Englanders had their own hybrid lore and 'receipts'. Strings of dried corncobs were hung about the kitchen as fertility symbols, and local baking recipes invented. The latter included such inimitable pioneer delights as johnnycakes (from 'journeycakes' for the workers who took them with them to the fields), the beach clam-bake, and Boston baked beans. Many Australian Aboriginal women in seminomadic communities still make 'dampers', a robust bread made from wild grass seed and baked in the white ash of the fire.

Kitchen Character

Whatever the season, a thoughtfully designed kitchen is an inviting place that is a pleasure to be in. Characterful kitchens, the sort that recall the countrified kitchens of childhood books such as Laura Ingalls Wilder's *On The Banks of Plum Creek*, where Ma's new kitchen was 'clean and piny' with a shiny black cookstove whose 'doorknob's little iron tongue clicked', are often full of freestanding mismatched furniture. The point is, the pieces,

A glass-roofed conservatory or house-extension, or even a large skylight, is a wonderful medium through which to listen to the musical patterns of the rain, especially when sharing a meal with friends and family. This example, made entirely from glass, is built onto a 1950s red-bricked house in London.

whether heirlooms or eclectic re-painted junk store finds, are loved and practical, however eccentric.

Large, practical, and beautiful work-surfaces are all-important for people who cook a fair amount. A fine hardwood such as beech, elm, or cherry is wonderful to work on, and was much favored for its exquisite simplicity by Puritan home-makers. If you are choosing stone the ruggedly organic quality of granite, a naturally even heat spreader, is the ultimate choice for the area right next to the stove.

Stove Choices

People make a lot of fuss about stoves. Personally I like an old-style range, with its even distribution of heat, but I've eaten memorable meals from two-ring electric stovetops in white-washed cubby holes on Greek islands. The quality of the ingredients and the craftsmanship and imagination of the cook matter more than the *suavité* or historic authenticity of the stove. Whatever your food philosophy: macrobiotic (a Far Eastern régime balancing yin and yang, masculine and feminine principles in food), vegetarian, Muslim, Jewish, omnivore … if you enjoy cooking, the end result will taste good.

Kitchen Furniture

Housewives, of necessity, in days of old (and indeed in many parts of the developing world today), had to to keep their *batterie de cuisine* in good condition for a lifetime, so they had to make sure it was of good quality in the first place. So the expense of a few good-quality, copper-based saucepans is worthwhile and infinitely preferable to a whole roomful of cheap, thin, and badly enameled ones.

This philosophy of surrounding yourself with beautiful, useful things should extend to the dresser. Utilitarian modern appliances such as refrigerators and freezers seem to fade into the background if they are surrounded by characterful cupboards. If you don't have a dresser, create the same effect by nailing up some shelves above a chest of drawers and painting them the same color. The artifacts, dishes, cups, and bowls arranged on it should be an interesting miscellany of shapes and patterns – a sort of personal museum of given and chosen objects. Cracked perhaps, chipped maybe, but loved and used nonetheless.

Dining Ambience

Ulysses, after finishing his epic voyages, was rather partial, it seems, to 'endless dishes' washed down with 'unceasing cups of wine'. This formula, with variations in moderation in the 'endless' and 'unceasing' department, has been popular with diners ever since. The ritual of dining has, though, on the whole, always been as much about the ambience and the company as it has about the menu; a sort of touchstone for affir-

This kitchen in an old rectory in Oxfordshire, England, has been renovated by a Danish couple, and shows off classic Scandinavian taste for simplicity and confident color purity.

mation of self and relationships. This need for human connectedness has often had a spiritual aspect. The Native American 'whooparla', or food-share, traditionally offered a thanksgiving portion to the gods, while the Ancient Egyptians drank from lotus-shaped cups made from lapis lazuli, emblem of the heavens and seed of the stars.

The 'Groaning Board'

Of vital importance if you are going to eat inside in either the kitchen or the dining room, and you're not going to sit on thick rugs on the floor Indian- or Middle Eastern-style, is a reasonably sized simple, solid table. Space dictates the dimensions – in a small apartment the table often has to double up as the countertop. A round table invites cozy conviviality by physical proximity and the lack of any particular 'head' of table. A long refectory table edged by humble benches or pews gives a monastic air or feel of an Italian street party. If possible position your table close to a large window or french doors so that you can commune with the outdoors, or when weather permits take it outside for al fresco-style dining. Always have a seasonal nature-inspired table centerpiece; flowers or array of fruits and vegetables.

Surprising Settings

The elements of surprise and inner-childish delight should not be forgotten when setting the table. The wine and water glasses could be in different colors … shells, flowers, and homemade brightly wrapped candy dotted around in doll-sized saucers. Rose-petals could float in finger-bowls at a hands-on meal. Napkins could be tied with rough string, ivy, clematis stems, or braided leaves, or child-size rainbow Indian glass bangles used as napkin rings.

Buy an old-fashioned calligraphy pen and some scented ink and use your best copperplate to make place cards out of recycled rag/plant and flower fiber paper. Use paper plates and paint dots and swirls on the edges with vegetable-based paints or dyes, or transform cabbage leaves, patty-pan squashes, melon-halves, and the like into impromptu plates and bowls. Whatever you decorate with, make sure it is illumined with candle-power – either on the table floating like a votive flotilla in a water-filled, shallow dish, or glittering above or near by in a Moorish lantern, rustic candelabrum, or treelike, silver-cupped menora.

The Crisp Cloth

Let your tablecloth be a crisp snowy wimple-white or a food-suggestive hue … crushed strawberry pink, for example, or lettuce-leaf green. Embroidered Indian materials or lightweight (clean!) Oriental rugs give your table an atmospheric baronial feel for a special occasion. In Provence no well-dressed table is seen without three 'skirts' – the first colored, the second lace, and the top layer a transparent veil of organdie. Meals outside are great fun, but if you want your tablecloth to stay put on a windy day, weight it down with spirals of seashell and holed pebbles tied to tough twine.

Picnics – Indoors and Out

Some of the most memorable meals are picnics. These, of course, don't have to be held outside – a picnic on a rug on the living room floor on a cold windy day can be highly entertaining! The outdoor picnic tradition originated in Europe in medieval times with pilgrims' wayside meals *en route* to their chosen shrine.

By the eighteenth century the gentry were so worried that inclement weather would spoil their great hooped dresses and satin breeches that they dotted little Arcadian pavilions around their grounds to dive into if it rained. The pavilion idea is not a bad one and neither is the antique idea of eating flowers. Early European recipe books are full of sugared and vinegared flowers; and rosewater, still very much used in India and the Middle East in cooking, was a very common ingredient in puddings and confectionery.

This recipe, from *The Compleat Cook*, 1655, is for Taffity Tarts – an ideal sweetmeat to take on picnics. 'First wet your paste with Butter and cold water and roule it very thin, also then lay them in layes and betwen every laye of apples strew some apples and some lemond pill, cut very small. If you please, put some Fennel seed to them; then put them into a hot oven, and let them stand an houre or more, then take them out and take Rose-water and Butter beaten together and wash them over the same and strew fine sugar upon them, then put them in the Oven againe, let them stand a little while and take them out.'

Healing Hospitality

Sharing food, thoughts, and emotions is an age-old human healing ritual for damaged relationships; but it is not just the stuff of legend that for some small close-knit family groups, calendar holidays, birthdays, weddings, religious celebrations, and the like can be unbearably stressful. If however we are open-minded, welcoming, and include people in our tribe who are distant relations or not relations at all we might just find that the changed dynamics of our extended social group are beneficial to all.

'The house of a friend is the best of all houses.'
Traditional

'Let your food be your medicine, let your medicine be your food.'
Hippocrates

be & do

There is a world of difference between quietly but positively just 'being' and doing blissful nothing, and listlessly wandering from room to room wondering what to do next. The difference is a state of mind. One person may decide to succumb to the Pleasure Principle and spend half an hour concentrating on really experiencing the lovely small evidences … heartbeat, pulse, sensations of hot or cold … of existence. Another person has a time-package with no activity ticked off against it … and this is a cause of anxiety and guilt, for he or she is locked into a mind-set that sees frenetic busyness as a measure of worth. Many contemporary lifestyles lack those necessary voids when individuals can just sit and think, or wallow in the luxury of not consciously thinking at all.

Yoga is an excellent introduction to the technique required for just sitting and 'being' in a relaxing, stress-defusing way. Even if you do not wish to get involved in formal yoga classes, simple deep breathing is an excellent calming technique for the nervous system.

It is in these quiet, solitary moments, far removed from the frenetic pressures of work, that we are reminded of the wonder and beauty of the immediate environment: the texture of wood for example, or the rhythmic drumming of rain on a windowpane. In these 'vacations' from our intellect our senses reveal everyday things to us anew.

When people think of physical 'doing', they often think of strenuous exercise such as working out in the gym. Brisk walking is, in fact, one of the best forms of exercise there is, and has the advantage of enabling you to observe the changing seasons and weather and enjoy social interaction with others. Feeling part of a diverse community of individuals who are all getting on with 'being' and 'doing' in their own personal way, is an uplifting experience.

At home of course we seem to never stop 'doing' … most of it mundane homemaking stuff. So it lifts the spirits to give yourself tiny kindly treats and whimsical entertainments as you go along … a bag of candies, a fun message on the freezer, the promise of an imminent long, hot soak in a violet-scented bath.

It is also incalculably good for the soul to have an ongoing creative Grand Project on the mental drawing board, whether planning a trip to Greenland, writing a novel, building a bower out of bamboo canes, knitting a vast, multicolored dream-coat, or throwing a summer party in a garden tent, cunningly disguised for the occasion as a medieval pavilion.

No matter how beautiful or serene our physical home environment, how meaningful its decorative ephemera, or authentic its historical resonance, the most potent memories we will have of it will be of states of being – of activities, conversations, and repose within the shelter of its boundaries. Home is the safe haven where we try out aspects of personal change and development: new hobbies, new hairstyles, or new philosophies. Home is where we unravel and try to understand the different strands of our complex personas through verbal interchanges, as well as in silent contemplation in solitude.

Creativity and Enjoyment

The most welcoming, individualistic homes and rooms are those in which the occupants express their unique character through a variety of particular skills and interests. Talent or lack of it is not the point here, creativity and enjoyment are. The positive energy conjured by eager 'doers' is made visible by multicolored balls of knitting wool, salt dough wreaths awaiting glazing, the half-finished canvas, sheafs of paper covered with tumbling thoughts and dreams, the borrowed bassoon by the music stand, the junk-store material in the sewing machine, the scented geranium cuttings awaiting re-potting in a tray. No amount of expensive décor can impersonate the raw appeal of busy, homely satisfaction, just as the most sophisticated electronic entertainment cannot ultimately recreate for us the simple magic of being and doing.

In order for our homes to function rewardingly, we have to understand the intrinsic purpose and meaning of all our living spaces … from the important age-old welcoming function of the porch and hall to the relaxing 'be yourself' ambience of the living room. Similarly we must realize that in any family group, be it small or large, the individual's need for privacy and personal space must be utterly respected if communal 'togetherness' rituals such as mealtimes are to be a harmonious interchange of ideas and feelings.

After all, being alone creatively – whether in meditation; reading a personally transformational book; contemplating what Longfellow called 'the secret anniversaries of the heart' – is a powerful and emotional business. It is utterly reliant on the sensitivity of others to one's need for spatial apartness. And it is in these ordinary, pearl-like moments of quiet, memory, and hope that we are given the inner refreshment and 'lift' which enables us to make a significant contribution to improving our everyday surroundings and our relationships.

The Work of a Home

Think of all the complex, varied work your home has to do. It must formally observe comings and goings; provide the right ambience, stimulus and asylum, for talking and silences, play and work … all through the moods and needs of the seasons. 'Home' includes not just the house but outdoor areas such as a balcony or patio. For not only does this patch of nature add a touch of the wild divine to the dullest of urban or suburban landscapes, it can provide a living space that links outside and inside like a permeable membrane. Our daily round, then, can be a hymn to living as opposed to mere existence, to potential instead of shortcomings. Simple, instinctive shoe-string style with a natural feeling can be a hundred times more chic and delightful, after all, than a houseful of pretentious glitz.

Transitional Space

Those fortunate enough to have a roomy porch, portico, or veranda outside the front door can make the most of this transitional, pausing area with a traditional southern American swing or a couple of rocking chairs. Place big pots of rosemary nearby to scent the air as you swing and ponder. This herb, sacred to the Virgin Mary in Southern Europe, symbolizes love, remembrance, and friendship. A clematis twining near the swing would also be pleasantly soporific – this is the plant whose very presence conjures the dream-world for the Iroquois people.

Neither In Nor Out

The threshold itself has always been of great significance in all cultures. Neither in, nor out, of the dwelling, it is generally consid-ered folklorically to be a dangerous spot from which the householders need protection. The Balinese guard the inner courtyards of their family compounds with magical carved figures such as the Cosmic Turtle, while Hindus place statues of the elephant-headed god Ganesh by their front doors. Yoruba African tribespeople traditionally cover their doors with an intricate carved lattice-work to keep out undesirable spirits, while Tunisians ring their doors with lines of 'magical' indigo blue paint.

In the West in modern times this protective threshold role has atrophied and become a 'guardian' doorknocker – often a snarling lion, a talismanic female hand, or a 'lucky' horseshoe shape, originally sacred to the Celtic horse god-dess, Epona. Many people who have bay trees in pots on either side of their doors do not realize that this is a very ancient European household protec-tive practice – bay was renowned for deflecting both witchcraft and lightning. Sacred in Ancient Greek times to the god of poetry and prophecy, Apollo, the bay was said to grant the wishes of those who wrote their heartfelt desires on its leaves of good fortune.

The Welcoming Hall

The role of the hall in any home is not to impress or intimidate but to make guests feel immediately at home. In Italy it is tradi-tional for a big terracotta pot of fragrant, vivid green basil to sit on the hall table as a symbol of welcome to visitors, who may later eat some of its sweetly intense leaves in a homemade pesto sauce accompanied by pasta.

Make a therapeutic 'welcome potpourri' from not only lavender but also clary sage, noted by aro-matherapists for its euphoric, antidepressant qualities; as well as strongly scented rose petals, believed to be both emotionally and physically healing. Ring the seasonal changes in your 'welcome potpourri' with additional unusual dried flowers and seed-heads, and appropriate essential oils such as warm, anxiety-relieving sandalwood or sweetly spring-like stress-busting geranium. Put your inspirational concoction into a big blue bowl – for this is the hue to lower the pulse rate and make people feel they are in a safe harbor.

Whether your hallway is a bright, airy passageway or a tiny, mysterious cupboard arrangement, the newly arrived visitor should be able to catch tantalizing glimpses of other interior roomscapes beyond – through doors slightly ajar, or heavily draped portière curtains swagged across archways and entrances. Don't forget to make the most of the innate mystery of the hall, whatever its size, when entertaining in the evening. Fill shallow glass bowls full of glittering nightlight candles to pierce the shadows, or invest in a striking ceiling-hung candelabra, antique or contemporary, to cast subtle pools of light on arriving and departing guests. Avid recyclers, those priests of pragmatism

How much more sensual and atmospheric it is to come into a hall with polished natural wood or stone floors dotted with lovely, faded old rugs than into a bland, utilitarian foyer or entrance lobby carpeted with synthetic materials. Simple, pure beeswax polish is a memorable, evocative smell for a hallway, and so is the fresh pungency of calming lavender. This inviting hall is in a house located in Les Baux, France.

and visual poetry, make their own organic candelabra from branches of sun-bleached driftwood to which nightlight-filled jam jars are attached with wire, or utilize gilded bicycle wheels or children's hula-hoops cleverly fitted with candle sconces. Make your hallway sing with welcoming words by using découpage techniques or freehand to adorn the walls with appropriate poems, sayings, and mottoes in flowing calligraphy.

Alluring Vistas

Those arriving at the front door of some small cottages, summer beach houses, and garden apartments can catch an alluring telescopic vista of the back garden or terrace down the passageway through the open back door. Some may worry about the 'escaping energies' in this straight-through hallway scenario, but a home-made door-screen of shells on strings and/or glass beads will combat that problem, as will a transparent sari door curtain.

Don't make invitees crane their necks like giantess-sized Alice in Wonderland gazing at the Queen of Hearts' garden through a miniature door. Give them a glass of wine and trot straight through to your tousled orchard/seashore

In the garden room – the home's transitional sanctum – it is important to keep clutter to an absolute minimum, and have doors and windows unobstructed by physical obstacles such as curtains, blinds, or hanging baskets, giving direct physical and visual access to the garden proper.

grove/minimal rooftop garden eyrie. Some researchers have claimed that plants thrive best where there is an abundance of classical music and gentle conversation, while *feng shui* devotees say that in any area which can be loosely called a 'garden' both plants and people flourish when proper windchimes – precision-tuned to ensure their tonal quality – tinkle melodiously in the background when there is a slight breeze. For many centuries windchimes have been an integral feature hanging from trees in the gardens of Far East temples. Their harmonious sound is believed to both promote tranquility and ward off spirits of ill fortune by catching passing flows of positive energy and causing them to linger in the garden.

The Garden Room

Yellow is a positive color favored by *feng shui* practitioners for garden rooms – this does not have to be the overall color but can be picked out in highlights and objects, from flowerpots to ornamental rows of gourds. Tiny, twisted bonsai trees are also believed to be power houses of positive energy, and fish tanks, especially with mirrors behind them, brim with good auguries, as does any sort of moving water ... there are some charming, very inexpensive, urn- and jar-based 'fountains' available fitted with small electric pumps. The garden room is thought to be an optimum place for offloading the stress and strain of everyday life – a sort of land-based decompression chamber.

Mind Journey Markers

A gently meandering path in the garden is another *feng shui* plus. Soothing, elegant Japanese gardens often make use of stepping stones over streams and water features, or metaphorical water of raked gravel. These markers emphasize the concept of the garden as a sort of 'mind journey', as do a variety of seats (stones, tree stumps, rough benches, swings) found in unexpected spots. Dividing the garden into different mood and activity 'rooms' is a perfect way of ensuring that you, your family, and visiting friends all get nature-communing time together and separately as required. This 'hide-and-seek' concept works well even in the most minute garden area. Collections of stones: sculptural rounded shapes smoothed by water, or sharp flints once attached to seashells or ancient fossils, can be used creatively in your home in great sculptured heaps, in winding pathways, or in courtyard designs such as those favored by the villagers of the Dodecanese Islands of Greece. Similarly the textures and subtle colors of primeval ammonite fossils, as well as stones and pebbles (and the lichens that grow on them), can be highly inspirational. Use huge stones indoors and out as table tops and seats;

A living room in a house (overleaf) in Amagansett, Long Island. The ground floor has been opened out into a single area, with massive through fireplace heating both the living area and the main bedroom. This is an example of how the colors and textures of the outdoors can be used to good effect in an indoor environment.

make drystone walls around your backyard. Some native peoples believe that such stones are storehouses of energy, and, certainly, on many old standing stones throughout the world are carved the spiral symbol of power and creativity.

Al Fresco Eating

The terrace or deck outside the back door is a practical place to have a table for al fresco eating and barbecuing (from the Hawaiian 'barbacoa' – cooking outside). Cooking out of doors on a barbecue, no matter how small, is another way of enjoying the primitive pleasures of fire-making. Zoroastrians still believe that the world will be redeemed and transfigured by a divine fire, and burn fires in sacred cauldrons during their worship. Shiva, the Hindu lord of the cosmic dance, carries a consuming flame in one of his four hands.

For many peoples, including Hindus, Native American Plains tribes, the Mayan, Inca, and Aztec cultures, as well as the Celts of Europe, fire represented the power of the sun. Plains Indians still hold a Sun Dance each summer, in which dancers whirl around a pole whose sacred geography is meant to represent the world axis.

As a focus for outdoor sustenance, if you haven't already got a big garden table, make an impromptu low version out of an old door resting on four big upturned terra-cotta flowerpots, or, if you're feeling more artistic, make a personalized mosaic tabletop using earthenware teaplates or tiles. For safety's sake don't forget to cover the front of the plates with adhesive tape and sandwich them between two pieces of cardboard before smashing them with a hammer.

Herbs, Vegetables, and Flowers

A small graveled area can be transformed into a formal herb garden and vegetable *potager* with the assistance of planking to turn the central area into a raised bed. A French eighteenth-century look can be achieved by arranging the planking surround into a star pattern, an Elizabethan English tapestry feel with box or hyssop topiary in pots in the center and on the corners of the bed … either spheres or cones or bird-shaped standards. Here you can plant the herbs and flowers essential for homemade potpourri and do-it-yourself household potions, relaxing tisanes and elixirs, incense and pharmacopoeia: lavender, rosemary, mint, southernwood,

Rustic cabins, garden grottoes, an idyllic treehouse or earthy potting shed, a studio cabin, or a den in the tangled bushes. Such creations have always answered our human need for a hideaway. Perhaps a practical and symbolic space like this, which links outside and in, can become an escapist retreat for anyone who needs it (see also p.100). This garden house, on the shores of Lake Garda, Italy, belongs to a five-year-old child.

Taking the inside out (overleaf) … spending a short time relaxing amongst the greenery is a perfect way of recharging the batteries once more.

camomile, lemon balm, bergamot, sage, scented geraniums, rue, tansy, thyme, pennyroyal, catnip, clove pinks, borage, Sweet Joe Pye, sweet violet, and of course roses and the tissue-papery flowers of the cistus plant.

Backyard Kitchen Gardening

Even those who only have room for a few sink gardens can grow herbs, and indeed fresh vegetables, fruit, and edible flowers and greens as a worthwhile nod in the direction of self-sufficiency. As many urban community gardens around the world demonstrate – creativity and fun are all when it comes to small-scale horticulture using low-cost materials. People plant cabbages and dramatic sea-kale in discarded truck tires, lettuce and nasturtiums in holey old buckets, runner beans scramble up tall, thin bamboo-pole tipis sunk in gaudy olive-oil cans.

Wildlife Gardening

Of great importance to children's understanding of the natural world is the establishment of a wildlife garden of some sort. Adults also love observing the bird table, the bat-box, the buddleia butterfly bush, the insects in the native plant patch, and the wetland habitat … even if it is just an old sunken baby bath housing two frogs, some weedy water, and a host of daphnia. Chemical insecticides, weed killers, and fungicides are, of course, a complete no-no for anyone wanting a nature-sympathetic, ecologically sound garden. Have a sundial in your garden to tell the time by the shadows cast by the sun, and a little tree (perhaps an elder, traditionally possessing powerful protective magic), hung with interesting found objects and fluttering wish and prayer rags tied on by family and visitors.

Natural Screens

You don't have to divide your personal paradise with permanent hedges. Screens made of bamboo poles tied together or willow hurdles can create useful instant garden 'rooms' where people can do their own thing.

One person might be reading, a couple of others playing ball on the lawn, another having a quiet think under some shady trees … all in adjacent 'compartments'. Some Eastern religions uphold that individual trees and plants are in fact nature spirits or 'devas' made visible – choose the area with the most beautiful 'devas' for your thinking bower.

Make a raised flower-bed 'seat' of softly scented camomile, as they did in the Middle Ages, or a chair out of living willow withies that sprout when you anchor them in the ground. Perhaps a mini-labyrinth or circular spiral made of flints and shells could enhance the quiet corner. In medieval times walking a maze or labyrinth was seen as symbolic of an inner journey, a substitute for an actual pilgrimage to a holy shrine.

Reserve a warm, dry corner for your pet's bed. Choose a spot so that it is not likely to be tripped over or poked constantly by little children (see also p.102).

Let your personal work space delight and entice you. Fill it with ordered chaos of color and contrasting textures and treat yourself appreciatively. Make yourself a tray of herbal tea or good coffee, complete with trimmings like a delightful cup and saucer, a pot of organic honey, a dish of homemade cookies. Light a stick of your favorite incense, put on some soothing background music ... and let the inspiration flow (see also p.107).

Sacred groves of trees were the contemplative nature worship sites chosen by the Ancient Greeks, the druids and some Native American peoples.

Few of us are lucky enough to have a full-scale grove growing in our garden, but even on a modest patio you can put trees that are special to you in pots in a mini-avenue. Australian eucalypts, for example, are not only evergreen, they are highly aromatic and therapeutic for many household and medicinal purposes. They are considered magical in Aboriginal mythology, in which they are sacred to the moon.

Water Music

A very shallow stream (recycled by a pump if you haven't got a natural one), could provide the necessary romantic, uplifting sound of water as well as a place to paddle and sail paper boats on a hot day. (Small children should always be closely supervised when they are playing near even shallow water.)

Children adore tents, tree platforms, and playhouses ... when they eventually lose interest in the latter adults may want to colonize them ... the playhouse, painted with the All-Seeing Wisdom Eye of Buddha, becomes a meditation stupa, a miniature summerhouse for rainy teatimes, or a tiny art studio (see also pp.94-5).

The pointed shape of a stupa or pavilion can be echoed by turning half an abandoned old upturned rowing boat on end and making it into a garden wayfarer's shelter ... in Japanese garden symbology this pointed shape represents the cleansing qualities of a mountain. Put round 'portholes' in the side in the style of Zen monastery 'moon windows'.

Transformational Places

Even 'ordinary' garden sheds are wonderful transformational places when just filled in traditional style with tools and dusty seed packages ... but these bosky structures can also become ideal places to practice that challenging piece of music or rehearse amateur theatricals, house a potter's wheel, or a woodworking bench.

Those who have no garden space need not despair ... they can turn the wall outside their sunniest window into a wonderful glassless greenhouse. Hang colorful tin cans and pots on nails outside your window, fill them with vegetable, herb, and flower seedlings, and watch as the heat stored in your walls produces a cozy microclimate to nurture your Hanging Gardens of Babylon.

Personal Space

Organizing the space inside the house to give everyone their own space takes ingenuity and imagination in equal measures. The space allotted to each individual, after all, must not only have the right physical parameters but also the right atmosphere to suit each personality. Dovetailing to these dynamics often requires a complete rethink of the way we use our homes. For example, as the conceptual line between indoors and outdoors becomes blurred, so we can make it more indistinct by bringing 'incongruous' plants and trees inside the house in pots – including small fruit trees and ornamental vegetables. Even if we haven't got the right amount of light to turn our homes into giant conservatories, we can

make a significant gesture toward 'bringing the outside in', and reap the mood and health benefits living with greenery and its 'living climate' bring.

Double Uses

Using this new mind-map of your house beneficially often means change and/or compromise. Don't put off all those creative things you want to do because you 'haven't got the space'. If you don't have a big home, a light, bright conservatory-kitchen, for example, can double up as a craft/artwork studio with use of some clever storage. Paint some wooden vegetable crates from the market (you can put castor wheels on the bottom), or use attractive baskets that stack on top of each other. Get two vegetable carts or racks, one for the potatoes and carrots, another for your needlepoint/oil paints/manuscript of novel-in-progress/sewing machine and soft furnishing stores' discontinued sample books of material (ready-made patchwork squares!).

Warmth and Bustle

The kitchen should be warm and full of bustle – not an antiseptic laboratory, even if it does boast state-of-the-art appliances. Celebrate the commonplace here. Don't hide your nicest cooking utensils away – display them proudly. Your *batterie de cuisine* may be well and truly battered, but its decrepitude is its endearing badge of office (see also pp.72-3). Encourage family and friends to use it. Children enjoy stirring the pan and visiting adults feel at home if they can

101

chop and grate whilst talking. If you have a little cubby hole in this practical and emotional engine room of the house – put in a little bowl of rice and a few flower petals in honor of the Chinese kitchen god, or thanksgiving icon of your choice.

If you are lucky enough to have an old-fashioned wooden washing pulley over a solid fuel stove in your kitchen, don't just discreetly dry your laundry on it, or festoon it with purely ornamental garlands. Use it – to dry children's artworks; culinary and household herbs (hung upside down in brown paper bags); strings of chilis; and flowers suitable for dried-flower arrangements such as statice and sea lavender.

Secure Pets

A solid fuel stove is, of course, a natural gravitational spot for household pets. If you don't have a constantly cozy stove remember that pets, too, need a special 'secure' place of their own to snooze and dream in (see also pp.98-9). Make a dog or cat bed using nonsweaty washable cotton or a nonchemically treated fleece –

The fireplace is an important focal point in any living room, as in this English Cotswold cottage, which dates back to the 17th century. Since fire was first made by chilly, curious cave persons, human beings have wanted to sit close by it for its relaxing heat as well as its vision – inspiring light and colors. It is important, therefore, to create inviting and comfortable seating next to the hearth, in this case high-backed Dutch chairs.

wash it regularly and put several drops of tea-tree or eucalyptus oil in the rinse water to repel fleas. A few drops of these oils rubbed into an animal's collar is an additional natural way to keep pests at bay, as is a mattress filled with tansy and pennyroyal. Make cat naps even more blissful by making up some soft little sleep-pillows filled with down or kapok, catnip, and valerian.

Mezzanine Magic

Humans needing their own space in a house with limited floor area but high ceilings can often be imaginatively accommodated by making a mezzanine level in the room, using sustainable timber, organic glues and natural resins, paints, and polishes. These areas are ideal for making a home-library, complete with old-fashioned stepladders.

This is the Age of Information, we are all too aware, but children and young adults should be made aware that there is far more to world knowledge than can be found through television, computers, and the Internet. Data overload and information chaos often result when children do not have a broad frame of reference with which to comprehend the extraordinary blitz of random electronic stimuli, utterances, and images with which they are bombarded on a daily basis. Books proffer a kaleidoscopic world of discovery with more depth and far more room for personal creative, imaginative input and emotional involvement. There should be no television or computer in the library area, just as many interesting reference and fiction volumes as you can lay your hands on (scour garage and rummage sales as well as secondhand bookstores and junkstores to fill the gaps in your shelves). Have some child-sized tables and chairs in the 'library', and plenty of scrap paper, pens, and pencils to encourage children to go there not only for homework purposes but for self-expression as well.

Useful Utility Rooms

A utility room is a useful spill-over for storage of messy children's play equipment such as poster paints and clay … make the room as bright, textural, and interesting as the rest of the house instead of utilitarian white to match the washer and drier. Look out for any item of furniture with lots of little drawers or niches – a set of old school lockers would be ideal – in which to store all the artwork clutter. The bonus is that littlies actually like to put things away in hideyholes! Turn the area by the sink into a miniature 'flower room' – store all your pretty, eccentric, or antique vases and unusual recycled jars in serried ranks on shelves over the draining board, along with plant misters and charcoal to keep the flower water smelling sweet.

Each room in Charleston, the English home of Vanessa Bell and Duncan Grant, is a visual testament to individual style. Murals cover the fireplace, complemented by offbeat sculpture, pottery, and a mixture of found objects and everyday clutter (see also p.107).

Every home needs a secluded corner for anyone who needs to take time out for private, solitary moments. This Mexican house, 'Home of the Happy Spirits', has just such a nook, complete with day bed and rustic corner hearth for complete coziness.

Room for Music

You may be fortunate enough to have a small spare room. If so, think about turning it into a music room where people can make dulcet, healing sounds or a terrible racket to their hearts' content without disturbing anybody. Cardboard egg boxes and egg trays stuck all over the walls and ceiling with the pointed bits facing into the room make good, cheap soundproofing. They can be painted vibrant colors to match the big, squashy floor pillows and sound-absorbent rag rugs you have provided. A box of cheap percussive instruments and wooden pan-pipes keeps visiting children happy for ages.

Quiet Work Space

The soundproofing is certainly important to anyone who works at home, which is an awful lot of us these days. Few have the luxury of a whole designated office to themselves – yet we need space and quiet in which to function properly. If you cannot migrate to the attic or a similar under-used area, a separate workplace can be arranged in most rooms with the help of a couple of folding screens and/or a vast old curtain draped from a couple of hooks on the ceiling. It is essential, though, that you have a table or desk that you love and a comfortable chair, ideally an ergonomically designed 'back chair', which properly supports the base of the spine in its ideal posture. A window that opens to let in fresh air and natural light is essential for health, as are nearby plants which lift our spirits and absorb pollution (spider plants are particularly well known for their effectiveness).

People using VDU screens should fit safety filters to reduce radiation and static. Many people find that using an ionizer helps to raise the level of beneficial negative ions in the air – as these are often destroyed by electrical equipment. Think of installing a small water feature just outside the office (but well away from electrical equipment); the sort with an integral pump. The sound of bubbling water on stone is relaxing, and constantly circulating liquid improves humidity levels.

Stimulating Work Space

Don't let your home work space be bland ... have a few beloved stones, small photographs, amulets, or ornaments on your desk/work surface ... a special pen, carefully sharpened pencils, a particularly beautiful lamp to work by, a music stand to prop your current reference books or documents on. Hang your favorite painting on the wall nearby (see also p.100).

Use the same kindly philosophy when you are 'living' in your 'living room', which often has to double up as the 'family room'. If the shapes of the furniture tend to be curved and organic the room will feel even more welcoming and 'safe' to all who use it ... angular shapes and hard lines can be somewhat threatening (see also pp.91-3).

Room for Cohesiveness

The ideal living room is a place where people not only relax but enjoy a multitude of activities together. This is not a call for the wholesale return of Victorian parlor entertainment but it is nevertheless good for the cohesiveness of any couple, or family group, to spend at least one night a week when they shut the television firmly in a cupboard and talk, joke, or even quietly do puzzles together! This is a room where everyone can have a say (and a hand) in the decoration.

A Testament to Individual Style

One of the most famous houses where adults have felt free to express themselves both socially and artistically is Charleston, Sussex, England, home to artists Vanessa Bell and Duncan Grant and their many visiting friends from 'The Bloomsbury Group'. In the dining room (complete with the important round table, so that everyone felt significant) visitors were made to feel involved in a creative continuum by being served from hand-painted plates and goblets.

Most important, the old house has lots of nooks and crannies where people could escape and think their solitary thoughts about things mundane and cosmic. This emotional and spiritual safety valve can be provided even in a relatively small home with some careful planning. Any recessed window can be fitted with a window-seat, so that someone can just pull the curtains and 'disappear'. Similarly, shadowy alcoves can be supplied with small armchairs, stools, or built-in benches; and lofts and mezzanine balconies furnished with some pillows and a skylight through which to observe the mysterious night sky.

'Let us, then, be up and doing.'
Henry Wadsworth Longfellow

cleanse

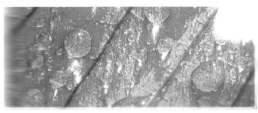

The subject of cleansing has always had many interpretations. The first and most obvious meanings are the ablution and bathing of the body, the soaking and soaping of clothing, and the sponging, sweeping, and disinfecting of the house. It has often meant more, though, than just these physical acts of hygiene and deodorization.

To be 'clean' has often also meant to be receptive and deserving of some sort of spiritual insight, and to this end it has been, and is common in many cultures, for purification rituals to be carried out in houses on a daily or weekly basis. These can take the form of lustration – the sprinkling of 'holy' water at the boundaries of a house, fumigation by incense, the uttering of magical charms, mantras, or religious prayers, or the writing of mystic symbols on walls or floor.

Many of us 'cleanse' our homes in the unconventional sense without realizing it. We do this even when we open the window to let in some fresh air – although we may not be aware of it, the act is often not so much to dilute the stale indoor air but to admit the energies of the natural world outside. We ritually 'cleanse' when we light a stick of incense, ignite candles or the fire – the ultimate symbol of purification – or spray the room with a plant mister scented with essential oil. The form of creativity that is homemaking has always required these small sacramental acts of its most passionate participants. We all know the wonderfully cleansing feeling of a clutter purge, of removing the ornamental evidence of a lifestyle and way of thinking which is no longer relevant to our current tastes and philosophies. Raking up the dead leaves on the lawn, going on a one-day fast, discarding clothes from a time when you were unhappy, painting a formerly hectically colored room serene white … these are all potent acts of cleansing.

Burning herbs and resins in the home is still thought to be spiritually and physically cleansing in some cultures. Scandinavians use them in the sauna, Arabian and African women perfume their newly washed hair in special 'smoke-tents'.

For most of us in the West, though, full immersion in water is the most desirable act of personal cleansing. The ultimate shrine to this act – the place where we not only wash and anoint ourselves but metaphorically slough off our outer skin like the selkie seal people of Gaelic mythology – is the bathroom. Fresh and vulnerable, we pamper ourselves in private, and hope to emerge scented and quite 'new'.

Bathing has always been a ritual not only of physical cleansing but also of spiritual purification, contemplation, and symbolic rebirth. Many mythologies consider water, with its links to the subconscious mind, as a 'doorway' to other worlds. Religious ceremonies often utilize water – immersion for baptism, to make holy signs and signatures on the human body, or to combine with 'holy' fire, to create lustrating steam to carry away sin and refresh the soul.

Bathing in the Past

Ancient Romans considered bathing to be a social occasion, with ablutions to be performed communally. As many as 1,600 people could enjoy the facilities at the Baths of Caracalla in Rome at the same time! The waters on offer were both cold and piping hot, thanks to the sophisticated hypocaust heating engineering of the day; they also had extensive underfloor heating in the bathing areas. The Romans often commenced their bathing rituals in the sudatorium, or 'sweat room', where heat was provided by wood-burning furnaces.

The use of steam for the well-being of both body and soul is common in Navajo and Plains Indian culture, where the supernatural 'sweat lodge' ceremonies are presided over by a shaman who pours water on heated stones to create the magic vapors in which mind and body are transformed into ascending spirit. New Zealand Maori peoples have used natural thermal hot springs in much the same way.

England during the seventeenth century was not known for its cleanliness or sweet-smelling qualities. Indeed, when Matoaka Pocahontas came to London from Virginia, where she was used to the Algonquin habit of daily river bathing, she was shocked by the general lack of personal hygiene. There were a few public baths in England at this time, inspired by travelers' tales of exotic Islamic hammam bathing, but they were looked on as something of a novelty. Here's an extract from Sir Hugh Platt's book *Delightes for Ladies*, 1651: 'I Know that many Gentlewomen, as well as for the clearing of their skins as cleansing their bodies, doe now and then delight to sweat. For the which purpose, I have set down this manner ... the steam of the pot passing throrow the Pipe under the half bottome of the bathing tub, which must be bored full of bigg holes, will breath so sweet and warm a vapour upon your body ... as that you shall sweat most temperately and continue the same a long time without fainting. Note, that the room would be close wherein you place your bathing tub, lest any sudden cold should happen to offend you whilest your body is made open and porous to the ayre.'

Uplifting Therapies

The ancient Indian healing system of Ayurveda also uses sweat therapy – *swedana karma*, a detoxification regimen utilizing oil massages, heated towels, and application of herbal pastes. This culture, though, has for thousands of years blended bathing, magic, medicine, meditation, and aromatherapy into an assortment of intriguing, uplifting permutations.

After a bath scented with rose-oil (it was Shah Jehan of Taj Mahal who first made oil of roses for his beloved wife Mumtaz when she exclaimed rapturously about the smell of the roses he floated on a lake on their wedding day), a well-to-do Indian woman calls for the *maalish-wali* to perform top-to-toe massage, oil her hair with jasmine essential oil, and do auspicious *mehndi* henna tattoos on her hands and feet.

Social Bathing

To the Finns, the timeless world of the sauna is a shrine to mind-body communion which climaxes, ideally, with a dip in an icy outdoor lake or pool. The Japanese passions for bathing still hinges on healing and the purification rituals of Japanese Buddhism. Bathing is also a highly sociable affair – Japanese people like to gather together outdoors in hot volcanic mineral springs, surrounded by romantically beautiful scenery. Indoors, at communal public bath houses, it is considered perfectly polite to wash first, before getting into the water. In both scenarios unselfconscious nakedness

A vigorous massage given by needles of piping hot water is highly sought after these days; the world's most popular being German state-of-the-art power-showers which are ergonomically designed, providing a wide range of angles. This example is in a house in Santa Monica, California.

111

is of the norm. Purist home bathrooms in Japan have deep, narrow heat-retaining, water-conservation-friendly, family-sized tubs made of smooth, aromatic *hinoki*, or cypress, wood. Ideally this kind of bathroom should have a dramatic floor-to-ceiling window which looks out onto a tiny, perfect courtyard garden.

Shower History

The earliest human shower experience was, of course, the experience of being caught out in the rain, or cavorting in a carefree manner under a small rockpool waterfall. The Romans tried to recreate the euphoria of standing under a torrent of water by establishing fountains dedicated to water nymphs in the hot pools of their bathing complexes. In Thailand and Indonesia the stone bathing pools of the royal court were decorated with intricate carvings of nymph goddesses, guardians of the stone waterspouts from which water gushed onto the heads of those wishing to commune with the water spirits.

Showers are, of course, more environmentally sound than baths, as they use far less water and can be fitted into awkward and inconvenient spaces in tiny apartments, where space is too limited to accommodate a full-sized bathroom; but the keen water conserver would still want to install a low-flow, water-saving, head. The ultimate in low-tech body rinses is the renowned Australian campers' outdoor bush shower, which consists of a large bucket of water and a cunning rope system attached to a tree.

Bathrooms as Sanctuaries

Bathrooms are the sanctum where tensions are dispelled in a miasma of hot, scented water. The healing qualities of natural fragrance allied with hydrotherapy easily soak away the stresses and strains of the day. It is important that you make this room into a completely relaxing refuge where you can sing at the top of your voice or lap up the silence in peace and tranquility. In spirit it should be as much like a natural watering hole as possible, containing shells, smooth pebbles, pieces of smooth driftwood, and damp-loving plants being the main decorative elements.

A simple, almost monastically empty, room with one large cast-iron roll-top tub positioned under a skylight so that the bather can lie in soft candlelit swirls of steam looking up at the stars – this surely is the ultimate in blissful experiences. Sybarites may wish to add armchairs, damp-proofed book cupboards (for who can deny the decadent delight of reading in the bath?), bath pillows, inflatable ducks, bath racks with inbuilt drinks trays – but the essence of the rewardingly tranquil bath experience is the old-fashioned long soak of weightless oblivion. Slap on a homemade botanical face mask of banana mash, relax … and emerge from your chrysalis a far brighter creature altogether.

A delightfully cool, all-over effect is achieved with these traditional Moorish bathroom tiles in a house in Morocco, producing an oasis of calm and practicality.

112

Rather than color and ornamentation, minimalists may prefer a plain white tub offset by beachcombings such as exotic shells, comforting sponges, strangely shaped pebbles and pieces of driftwood – alongside handsome bottles of bathtime unguents.

Treat your bathroom like a proper characterful room and pleasure shrine, not like a utility, and it will reward you a hundredfold. Old mirrors with the silvering wearing off lend an other-worldly air when covered with a fine mist of steam … old hip baths, recalling nineteenth-century fireside ablutions, can be reborn, with the aid of a pile of squidgy pillow, into quirkily chic bathroom chairs. Natural sponges, pumices, and loofahs piled high provide interesting shapes and tactile textures, as do piles of temptingly fluffy towels in palely pristine unbleached cotton or subtle vegetable-dyed tints. Retro-style wooden duckboard bathmats are, in fact, highly practical to use in the slippy bathside area as well as being esthetically pleasing. Some 'green' retailers now sell them in bamboo, the ultimate tough sustainable plant material.

Bathroom Embellishments

Shells, along with other nautically themed items such as fish and boats, are very positive symbols to have in the bathroom. They represent the feminine principle, fertility, rebirth, and good fortune; inner-shell spirals represent the very vortex of the cosmos, while fish of all kinds are associated with the moon, creativity, and the spiritual dimension.

Collect old crazed decorative wall tiles and put them up behind the bath and sink in pleasing color-themed mismatch. Alternatively, buy a witch ball prism or a batch of mirror tiles to turn your poky bathroom into a mystic ballroom. Turn an economically priced chain-store candelabra into something special for the bathroom by painting it white and wiring on some old glass lusters and/or Christmas silver ball decorations to reflect your candlelit watery idyll. Paint the room airy pure white, like a nun's cell, or give it a transparent glaze of blues, greens, and mauves to create a dreamlike underwater atmosphere.

Bathroom Nauticalia

Boats, meanwhile, are symbols of safety and security. Nauticalia, therefore, such as ships in bottles, shell mobiles, and murals featuring fish or mermaids (descended from the powerful

Semitic moon goddess, Atargatis), represent an affirming genre of ornamentation for your bathing sanctuary. So are moisture-loving plants, such as the many kinds of fern, which thrive in the humidity, absorb carbon dioxide, and release energizing oxygen into the air. The ideal greenhouse-bathroom opens onto a nature-space of some kind, which in warm climates could house an insulated solar-heated hot tub for sociable al fresco bathing with family and friends.

Whatever type of bath you use, whether it is standard, muscle-relaxing sitz, or whirlpool, you need, if possible, to recycle some of the bathwater to use on the garden, or at least the mini-tropical rainforest of houseplants on your bathroom windowsill. In the same conservation spirit you should make sure that your sink and tub faucets don't leak, and install a low-flush ecological water cistern in your lavatory, which would use half as much water as your current system.

Essential Oils and Fragrances

One of the greatest pleasures of cleansing our bodies is in using the wizardry of perfumed unguents and lotions. Fragrance is a potent restorative medicine and 'battery re-charger' for tired minds and spirits, and an array of revitalizing and soothing aromatherapy essential oils is a must for every bathroom cabinet. As English author Rudyard Kipling put it: 'Smells are surer than sounds and sights to make the heartstrings crack.'

The therapeutic qualities of aromatic oils extracted from plant material such as leaves, petals, fruit, bark, gums, and resins were used in antiquity by Egyptian, Arabic, Greek, Roman, Chinese, and Indian masters of medicine.

The simplest way to reap the benefits of essential oils these days is by putting a few drops in the bath water, so that you can inhale the hot scented water and let it be absorbed through the pores of your skin. This, then, has a deeply relaxing effect by sending calming messages to the brain's limbic system. However, there are warnings to take heed of. Essential oils are very strong and people with serious chronic health problems or allergies, pregnant women, parents with babies or very young children, and people taking homeopathic remedies should all consult a qualified professional aromatherapist before using essential oils. They should always be diluted and never taken orally.

Scour the junk stores and garage sales for beautiful old perfume or medicine bottles to put your own essential oil blends in, or recycle scrupulously washed-out vinegar or oil containers with interesting shapes. Dark glass colors such as green, brown, or blue best protect your oils from light (buy natural oils rather than choosing a synthetic product).

Blending and Choosing Oils

Choose oils whose scents best appeal to you, but when practicing this bathroom alchemy remember not to blend more than two or three, or the therapeutic chemistry of the oils may be changed. Always choose oils whose properties are sympathetic and complementary to each other. In a full bath, adults should use between five and ten drops of oil. Children enjoy a relaxing bedtime bubble bath using a couple of squirts of organic dishwashing liquid and three or four drops of lavender, orange, or camomile essential oil.

Recommended Bath Oils

Here are some of the most popular oils for adult bath use: Basil (stimulating, clears the head); Bergamot (uplifting); Chamomile (antiseptic, soothing); Eucalyptus (stimulating, decongestive); Frankincense (restorative, comforting); Geranium (harmonizing, warming, clarifying); Jasmine (relaxing, aphrodisiac); Juniper (muscle-relaxant, purifying); Lavender (healing, calming); Lemon (refreshing, anti-depressant, tonic); Neroli (aphrodisiac, anti-depressant); Patchouli (antiseptic, aphrodisiac, relaxing); Peppermint (muscle-relaxing, cleansing); Pine (stimulating, refreshing); Rose (soothing, relaxing); Rosemary (invigorating); Sage (relaxing, purifying, antiseptic); Sandalwood (sensuous, warming, sedative); Ylang-ylang (aphrodisiac, sedative).

In Hindu mythology the goddess Parvati not only anointed her body with perfumed oils with medicinal qualities but washed her person with floral and herbal essences. Similarly, European women from medieval times have used herbs and flowers in their washing water, homemade

Simplicity is used to good effect in this Japanese-style bathroom in London. The natural coir matting and slatted blinds complement a subtly hued pile of towels.

116

creams and soap, not only for their beautifying qualities but to absorb some of the magical properties the plants were thought to possess.

Here is a recipe for making 'Oyle of Camomile', from *The Good Huswife's Handbook*, 1588: 'Take oyle a pint and a halfe, and three ounces of camomile flowers dried one day after they be gathered. Then put the oyle and the flowers in a glasse and stop the mouth close and set it into the sun by the space of forty days.'

In Pharaonic days it was not uncommon for even less-than-wealthy citizens to sit about wearing exotic cones of scented wax on their heads, and anyone who had neglected to sprinkle musk on their clothes before a social engagement was considered most uncivilized. But then these were people to whom the aromatics were of paramount importance. They were used in all aspects of normal daily life: in religious rituals, in medicine, in beauty care, to perfume the home, and even to embalm the dead in preparation for the afterlife.

Nature's Bounty

Using nature's beauty store as our ancestors did can be as simple as putting a cheesecloth bag of deep-red fragrant rose-petals and jasmine flowers under the hot faucet when we run the bath (herbal tea bags can be a handy substitute if you're in a hurry); or in our own kitchen-apothecary making our own simple, wholesome shampoos, toothpastes, skin toners, and soaps from kitchen ingredients, essential oils, flowers, and herbs. Recipes from past centuries had

delightful ways of measuring the time-scale of stirring and mixing … one mentions the time spent saying the Ave Maria as being quite adequate, while another advises the intoning of 'the Misere Psalm very slowly'.

Sweet Water

Sweet washing waters distilled from rain or spring water and the petals of the garden's most fragrant flowers were once much favored by ladies of high rank in medieval castles, who sponged their faces from silver bowls.

As recently as the nineteenth century it was considered most welcoming in country areas for weary and dusty travelers to be greeted in their bedchamber by a bowl and a jug of well water sweetened using sprigs of rosemary and lavender. Alongside the bowl would have been a homemade floral wash ball made from carefully collected leftover scraps of Castile soap, oatmeal, rosewater, and assorted herbs.

Soap Scraps

Making your own soap from scraps can be a most creative recycling experience today. Perhaps even more beautiful than homemade wash balls are soap bars from scraps of pure humectant glycerine soap. These can be turned into luminous chunks by heating them in a double boiler, adding drops of essential oil and food coloring (plus a confetti of flower buds, poppy seeds, and citrus peels if you wish), and pouring them into a cutdown empty waxed carton. Here is an interesting nineteenth-century washing alternative. 'Delightful Toilet Bags' from *The Columbia Cookbook* should be: 'Filled with bran, grated olive soap and almonds, which, pressed in water a few seconds, give a creamy lather to be rubbed on the face, neck, and body, and wiped off with a soft towel, without rinsing.'

Splashing your face with cold rain water from a stone garden water stoop, or flow-form water-sculpture such as a Japanese sukebai, which pours out melodic liquid from different lengths of bamboo pipe, can be cleansing and energizing. On a hot day turn on the garden sprinkler or get a friend to train the garden hose on you (gently!).

House Spirits

When ordinary people believed that every house was guarded by protective spirits and gods, cleaning the house was as much a respectful religious duty as a matter of hygiene. Indeed, our word for scrupulous cleanliness comes from the Greek goddess Hygieia, daughter and assistant of the god of medicine, Asklepios.

Not to clean the hearth, the homely altar of the fire goddess Hestia/Vesta, was to invite ill-fortune. In later European cultures a folkloric assembly of fairies, hobgoblins, and brownies 'assisted' the housewife at her chores for a small nightly reward of a bowl of beer or cream left in the fireplace. Scandinavian supernatural domestic beings were called 'nisses', and were considered to be ancestral spirits.

Magical Assistance

Sometimes you probably feel as if you could do with a brownie to help with the household chores. Essential oils and herbs can in fact give almost magical assistance with housecleaning and laundry tasks, as is witnessed in the old household 'receipt books' that relied on them before synthetic chemical bleaches, disinfectants, cleansers, and deodorizers. Some of the latter are a veritable cocktail of irritants, others give off toxic fumes. Apart from not being health-giving to humans, the residues of some chemical substances, when discarded down the drain or plughole, are hazardous to the environment.

Make Your Own Polishes

Rather than reaching for the silicone-based aerosol spray polish, why not have a go at manufacturing your own aromatic woodshine? Start by grating some store-bought pure beeswax and gently heating it in a double boiler along with the same quantities of turpentine and olive oil and as many drops of essential oil of lavender as suit your sense of smell. Pour it in a pretty jar, pop in a few lavender heads, and label in your best handwriting with a fat-nibbed calligraphy pen. As you work up a sheen with your pol-

'Everything gets life from water' (overleaf), *The Qu'uran.* An indoor expanse of water fulfills our need for the calming, restorative qualities of nature's ponds, lakes, and streams.

119

ish you can drink in the scent of Shakespeare's 'flower of middle summer' and be aromatherapized into a daydream reverie. Luck-bringing lavender, associated with goddesses Hecate and Circe, has been used since ancient times to avert the evil eye and bring blessing on the home.

Cleansing Herbs

Other cleansing herbs which could enjoy a domestic renaissance in the pollution-conscious contemporary household include southernwood, much favored at one time by Pennsylvania Germans as a disinfectant and to repel flies and ants from kitchens and pantries, and sweet cicely, the big brown seeds of which were used to polish English and colonial oak floors and furniture in the seventeenth century.

Potpourris, using the myriad colors and odors of the garden, have a wonderful history. A different version in each room of the house adds background botanical mystique to the living space.

The flowers you use could proffer a symbolic message. Be imaginative and daring – mix deep-hued lilacs and hydrangeas; seedpods and dried leaves; wispy spring flowers and moss. Sweeten the air in the bathroom with hot lemon-juice down the toilet (it's a descaler as well as being a natural antiseptic), and continue the citrus theme with heaped spicy pomanders, oranges or lemons stuck with cloves in a dish on the cistern.

If you get used to garnering herbs, seed heads, and flower petals through the seasons you need never feel tempted to buy commercial potpourri, with its harsh synthetic odor, again. Experiment with making sleep pillows, herb pillows, and other soothing conceits. Gather all the plant material on a sunny morning and gently dry it, away from direct heat, in a shady but airy room.

Spring Cleaning

The ritual of annual spring cleaning has been around for a very long time indeed. It actually has clear magical origins in the many cleansing and purification ceremonies and rites of Imbolc, the Celtic festival marking the Earth's imminent vegetative renewal. After the process of house cleansing, doors and windows were thrown wide open to welcome in the new season of fertility, a magic protective circle of water was sprinkled around the homestead, and a candle was lit to symbolize the return of the sun after the long winter. The same religious cleaning dynamic was at work in yesteryear's Jewish households at Passover, when the women folk spread fine, clean golden sand on the floor, and hung pristine white curtains up at all the windows.

The best scent tonic for all of us is genuine fresh air filled with the nuances of nature. In this converted hammam, or bath house, in Beirut, windows are flung open for fresh air to enhance the invigorating aromas from the array of lemons.

Lavender and Rose

The twelfth-century visionary abbess Hildegarde of Bingen devoted a tract in her holy works to the benefits of lavender, much loved by the Romans as a washing herb (the word lavender comes from the Latin *lavare*, meaning 'to wash'). Hyssop, the Old Testament emblem of purity ('Purge me with hyssop and I shall be clean', said David), was a bee-beloved herb used throughout the ancient world as a temple broom and sprinkler for holy water.

For alchemists, the rose symbolizes divine love. It has also variously represented Isis, Venus, Vishnu, the Virgin Mary, and Freya. Today all of the aforementioned plants have been scientifically found to possess remarkable antibacterial, germicidal qualities, while lavender, along with frankincense, can actually stimulate cell growth.

Smudging

Native Americans use sage and sweetgrass herbs, as well as evergreen cedar needles, to burn ceremonially for their ritual 'smudging' purifications and healings of a space or person. You can gather and dry your own herbs (hang them upside down in a bunch in a dry, cool place), or buy pre-packed, ready-made smudge-sticks. The smoke from the herbs should be wafted toward the relevant person or area of the house. Always remember to observe fire-safety: light the herbs over a fireproof container, don't leave smoldering herbs unattended, and extinguish the flame after the herbs/sticks are lit.

In some countries people carry fragrance around with them – Indian and Balinese girls massage jasmine oil into their hair and braid the exotic blossoms (sacred to Vishnu) into their tresses. Bathing in scented water means that you leave a subtle but lingering aroma print behind you.

Symbolic Scents

For a quick-fix atmosphere buildup nothing beats incense, for which ready-made sticks are freely available. Some incenses have symbolic scents, such as the verbena of druidism, or the lotus of Ancient Egypt and Hinduism. Others provide perfume moods to complement the character or history of your rooms. We light incense, believing that our thoughts and prayers are carried aloft in the air to some sort of mystic receptor, and in many religions the dead are burned in the belief that some essence of the departed is wafted in the smoke to the care of the ancients and ancestors.

Scenting Your Home

Scent your naturally polished wooden staircase with the clean warmth of vanilla, for example; or fragrance your tiny mirrored, fire-lit dining room with rose and musk that are conducive to a 'tête-à-tête'.

In confined spaces, the Shaker house-cleaning habit of hanging the chairs on pegs on the wall in order to clean the floor unimpeded, is well worth trying. This picture shows a kitchen in a London mews house.

124

Perfuming a home in this manner seems a million miles removed from the harsh, sterile aromas of chemically based, ecologically unsound aerosol sprays. Some of the synthetic subliminal scents in our homes may actually be toxic and/or allergy-inducing. Therefore it is vital that we take steps to remove them or at least minimize their presences in our houses. We should make sure that the wood we use is not only sustainably produced but is also not treated with chemical pesticides and preservatives; that our materials and carpets are not giving off formaldehyde or other chemical residues; and that our paints and varnishes are based on natural, organic, and aromatic oils.

Disposing of our under-the-kitchen-sink chemicals that contribute to the 'sick house syndrome' becomes easier if we similarly start respecting our living space and visualize our homes as living organisms. After all, our concern for the environment at large begins right here at home. Life becomes much simpler (and cheaper!) when we stop being slaves to advertising and put house-cleaning in a commonsense historical context.

Green Great-Grandma

Thrifty, house-proud great-grandma was a goddess of green-ness without even knowing it. Among other things she used lemon juice and baking powder for cleaning out the stove; polished steel knife blades with a cut pota-

A feeling of immense satisfaction can be derived from a well-stocked cupboard of fragrant, fresh, crisp linen.

to; brightened her copper tea kettle with mixture of salt and buttermilk; wiped wood surfaces down with vinegar and water or cold tea; rubbed oil of lavender around the edges of the bookcases to keep mold at bay; and cleaned excessively greasy pans with cornmeal.

Commonsense Solutions

A holistic attitude to life is nothing new either. The nineteenth-century, Chicago-published *Woman's Exchange Cook Book* by Mrs Minnie Palmer advised readers to 'at all apportionments of time remember the Giver', alongside a tip to keep brooms soft and pliant by hanging them in a damp cellar. Apart from gratefulness to the creator, self-sufficiency and self-reliance were themes dear to the heart of Mrs Palmer and her hordes of avid readers – they had commonsense solutions to every conceivable household contingency.

Many of these tips and wrinkles are not only well worth trying today, they have a household history more ancient than even Minnie could have imagined. Her aromatic hint, for example, on how to get rid of household cooking smells by boiling a teaspoon of ground cloves or cinnamon in water for a short while has its origins in the medieval custom of fumigating cooking and other odors from the room by burning 'pastilles' of spices on a brazier by the hearth.

Using a pared-down, ecologically sound, cleaning kit does not mean that we want to re-institute the bad, time-wasting elements in our ancestors' lives. Few of us yearn to scour the floor with sand and ashes, for example. However, many of the natural products used in centuries past were actually effective and easy to use. Some, like the use of pure, unperfumed soap scraps in a bottle of water to make dishwashing liquid, are relevant to today's recycling ethos.

Disinfectants and Cleansers

White wine or cider vinegar and water in a pump dispenser makes a superb disinfecting cleanser for all types of greasy surfaces. A few squirts of vinegar or lemon juice in the hand-wash rinsing water makes those special plates and glasses gleam (bearing in mind that dishwashers should only be used when there's a full load as each cycle uses vast quantities of water). A refrigerator can be cleansed and given a tangy freshness by a wipe around with some halves of cut lemon, and the mold-free environment maintained by keeping a piece of charcoal inside it.

Stillrooms of the Past

European and colonial housewives also used lavender, rosemary, and thyme oil as a cleaner and disinfectant in bathrooms and toilets. To these venerable natural germicides we can add those marvels of the New World – eucalyptus and tea-tree.

Household store-rooms and still-rooms of the past, though functional by nature, must have also been very therapeutic places in which to gather up the cleaning materials for the day's housework. The wonderful mingled smells of pure olive soap, resin, almond oil, cardamom seeds, beeswax, rosewater, orris root powder, and all the sweet dried botanicals required to make air-freshening potpourris must have been ravishingly exotic.

Shaker Cleaning

The Shaker sisters knew for sure there was 'no dirt in heaven', and they made quite sure there was none in their communal dwelling houses by vigorous sweeping so that their spotless surroundings reflected their spiritual purity. The much admired Shaker peg-rails were in fact designed so that chairs could be hung up – giving the sisters' brooms ease of access to all floor areas (see also pp.124-5). Old European sweeping lore dictated that dirt should always be swept into the middle of the room before being gathered up in the dustpan, and that dust never be swept out of the front door for fear of sweeping out the family's good luck along with it.

Cleansing Clothes

With its implications of purification and renewal, laundry has always been surrounded with mythology, folklore, and religious ritual. From the reverent washing of clothing and household textiles in Indian 'sacred' rivers to seventeenth-century English country belief in hanging clothes out under the 'whitening' powers of the moon, household washing has always meant far more than mere cleansing.

In the creed of the Shakers it was meaningful that Mother Ann Lee, their foundress, had taken in laundry to support herself when she first arrived in the United States from England. For the colonial housewife in Australia, clean clothes on her children against the backdrop of the dusty outback were a matter of stubborn pride and a determination to succeed in the face of adversity.

Doing the laundry is not the usual way to write your creative signature. But by using floral vinegars, herbs, and essential oils in your final rinsing water you are giving your linen a very personal 'scent stamp', the way women have done in many cultures in centuries past. Take some time out from doing laborious hand-washing for some 'ye olde love' divination – float two corks in your washing bowl, if they float apart one or both of you is not committed to the relationship!

A White Wash

Like the Shakers, German, Dutch, and French women in particular have always been very fussy about the crisp whiteness of their linens. These days phosphates, fluroscar whiteners and brighteners, and bleach-activating agents (which may end up in our lakes and rivers and poison the fish by causing an imbalance of algae) are standard in many washing powders – but it's perfectly possible to achieve a clean wash using a ecofriendly powder.

You may have to add a water softener such as sodium bicarbonate or washing soda to get up a good lather in a hard water area, and if your wash is heavily soiled it is advisable to give it a presoak in borax (a natural mineral product), but these unscented substances are a great washing bonus if any of your family are allergy-prone.

Ecological Washdays

Energy-efficient, low-water usage, hot-fill method washing machines are now available on the market for those anxious about the fact that the average washing machine cycle uses 22 gallons (100 liters) of water.

Dry your laundry outside if possible and get the scent of the sun and air on it (unless you live in a very polluted area, that is!). Draping underwear or handkerchiefs on or near lavender or rosemary bushes is an old country scenting ruse which always works brilliantly.

Fragrant Storage

In many places – the Middle East, India, the United States, Europe, Australia – clean washing was often stored away in chests of aromatic wood, such as sandalwood, cypress, or cedarwood. If you don't have such a wood chest, you could buy pungent cedarwood blocks to put in with the dry washing to give it a forest scent and repel moths. Another old method of storage in French armoires, English linen closets, and the like was to make little 'sweet bags' from cheesecloth, silk, voile, or organdie filled with dried herbs and petals. Lavender, roses, cotton lavender, rosemary, costmary, woodruff, thyme, and hyssop were all traditionally used.

'I often think of that bathroom –
the water colours dimmed by steam
and the huge towel warming on the
back of the chintz armchair …'
Brideshead Revisited, Evelyn Waugh,
1945

'Wash thyself and thou shalt waxe shiny.'
The Leech Book of Bald,
900-950 AD

rejuvenate

Home is the place we return to after a day of hustle and bustle for a custom-made mixture of relaxation and invigoration, so we can cheerfully face the world anew tomorrow. This rest and recuperation is something we start looking forward to on the journey home … envisaging in vivid detail the cup of tea in the special mug, the ritual putting on of the slippers and the favorite piece of music, the calling of the cat for its supper. The rejuvenation actually begins the moment we begin this wonderful homeward-bound reverie.

On one hand the concept of 'resting' at home, and 'relaxing', is of course synonymous with putting one's feet up and enjoying an undisturbed nap or well-deserved deep sleep. It can also be just a reviving sit for half an hour in the sun on the patio, a spicy, scented soak in a bubble bath, a monumental blast through the headphones of your favorite opera/Gregorian chant/jazz band/Irish ceilidh music, a wander around the garden in a refreshing light rain shower. The whole idea of rejuvenation is that of self-nurturing; restoring and reviving oneself in order to cope with the demands of everyday life. More often than not those demands will revolve around the needs and problems of other people: work colleagues, children, partners, friends, complete strangers such as store assistants or transportation employees. In order to be proactive, helpful, and courteous to other people it's important to occasionally be kind to yourself! Some people are better at this than others. They recognize that they are exhausted and no good to anyone until they have restored their inner equilibrium. They relax by stretching out on the sofa with a good book, by lying on a rug under a tree, by languidly staring into the flickering flames by the fireside. There are those, meanwhile, whose idea of rejuvenation is to tackle something completely alien to their lifestyle and philosophy. These challenges are not 'rest' in the conventional sense; their restorative power lies in their refreshing difference to the norm.

Spare time horse riding, beach-combing, mountain climbing, making a traditional knot garden, singing in a choir … practicing all these 'part-time' talents, exploring exotic and previously unthought-of possibilities, can invigorate and lift the spirits for people with very different day jobs.

Many of us enjoy an extraordinary variety of activities … in our dreams. For the sanctuary of sleep remains the ultimate healer and restorer. It is a magic genie that transports us to strange and fabulous worlds and stories, the seedbed, often, of our as yet unmade creations.

The division of the march of time into day and night, action to rest and rejuvenation, has been mythologized in all cultures throughout the ages. Australian Aboriginal peoples believe that ancestor-spirits created the world by singing before turning into sleeping geographical features of nature, and that we humans are the 'spirit-children' living in their 'Dreaming'.

In this Dreamtime the totemic ancestors of various tribes emerged from their sleep in earth and roamed the continent, bringing natural features into being and naming them. This animist creation myth is also mapped by storytelling relating to certain configurations in the night sky, as it is for the American Pueblo Indians, for whom the moon and stars are supernatural beings.

The deification of the night sky, in particular the moon, occurred throughout the Middle East – where the moon was consecutively personified by the Mesopotamians, Phoenicians, Egyptians, and Greeks as the goddess Ishtar/Astarte/Isis/Hecate. The Greeks also had a goddess of the Night, called Nyx, who wore blue-black raiment and a filmy veil studded with stars. The bringer of dreams and sexual fulfilment, she was also the mother of Hypnos, the god of sleep, who looked after people's wandering souls while they rested.

The Moon's Importance

With its visible waxing and waning and potent effects on the tides and rhythms of human and animal life, the moon continues to be an object of superstition, folk magic, and awe for many otherwise urbane modern folk. The lunar links with soul, psyche, and sleep mean that the moon is thought to be a very favorable image to dream of, usually associated with love divination and fertility, and doubly lucky if moonlight is reflected on water in a dream.

The moon is also an emblem of personal growth and spiritual renewal and development, and some people feel that these qualities are enhanced if they sleep with a small dish of different-hued moonstones next to the bed. These lustrous stones were believed in old Ceylon, where they were found in abundance, to grow as a direct response to the rays of the moon and to possess all sorts of intriguing occult properties.

The Power of the Moon

European folklore has always associated moonlight with the activities of faery beings and magical happenings ... people still turn over silver coins in their pockets in moonlight in the light of a new moon in hope of future prosperity and revelers celebrating the annual harvest-home used to do the same to bring good luck.

Don't forget to make a wish as you gaze at the moon's reflection – a tradition common to many countries and cultures. The ancients believed that walking in moonlight was actually beneficial to health and happiness. The harvest moon was thought to be particularly powerful. At the full Moon in July, Buddhists celebrate Gautama's first relevation of the Wheel of Truth to his followers, an intimation of Enlightenment – Nirvana.

Dream Lore

Many who are very interested in dream interpretation keep a 'dream journal' in which they write down the often mysterious images and 'stories' from their unconscious the very moment they wake up. Sometimes, over a period of weeks and months, a fascinating pattern of dream messages and metaphors emerges, which can be reassuring, inspiring, or throw light on a long-repressed problem.

In some parts of the world it is believed that dreaming is actually another level of reality, and that our dreams are actually strands of memory from life existing in a parallel universe. For as Jung said, our collective unconscious or psyche has an ancestry that 'goes back many millions of years. Individual consciousness is only the flower and fruit of a season, sprung from a perennial rhizome beneath the earth'.

Bed Alignment

The canon of European, American, and Australasian folklore is divided on the lucky/unlucky alignment of beds. Some traditions demand that the bed be positioned in an east-west position to avoid nightmares; others say that is should be north-south. These days many eco-manuals, in fact, recommend that beds be placed in the latter position so that our bodies are restfully aligned with the earth's magnetic field, and that the bed frame and base be made of wood rather than magnetic metal, which can invite sleep disturbances.

A bright bedroom in the 'Home of the Happy Spirits', Mexico.

Bed Fashions

When Samuel Pepys ended his seventeenth-century diary entries with his famous phrase 'and so to bed', he evoked an image of a cozy four-poster with thick tapestry curtains, illuminated by the glow of a low fire in the hearth. A sense of enclosure, of protection, has been the major bedtime requirement in many cultures – in Scandinavia, eastern Europe, Russia, parts of France, and the Netherlands, for example, beds were often sited in warm down-

stairs living rooms inside shuttered alcove cupboards. Today people prefer a less stuffy sleeping
style, but often like the look and feel of being
inside their own private space – a 'relaxation envelope' – that signifies total retreat from the world.
Four-posters have come back into fashion, but
these days these canopied bed-islands are more
likely to be modern interpretations draped with
colonial-style wisps of material or diaphanous
tropical net tenting rather than heavy-duty dust-
catching drapes.

A Rejuvenating Haven

Some people like their bedrooms to be
ascetic and bare – a blank canvas against
which they can think and dream, allowing
the subconscious a clear run. Others like to be surrounded by a riot of colors, teetering piles of
books, and a nest-like clutter of familiar endearing
objects galore. Whichever style you choose, make
sure yours is a rejuvenating haven of tranquility, a
harmonious rest/sleep environment. Each of us
spends, on average, one-third of our lives in bed

Many people who are in retiring-from-the-world mode
feel, as the Rev. Sidney Smith did, that there is 'no furniture so charming as books', and turn their bedrooms
into a comfy mini-library with a wealth of imaginative
escapism and/or inspiration immediately to hand. This
16th-century Dutch house, a former convent, has its
bedrooms located under the steeply pitched, raftered
roof. Skylights and a door that opens at tree-top height
bring plenty of light in.

(that's about four months of each year!), and if we are to cope calmly with the stresses of everyday life and avoid illness, it is essential that both bed and bedroom provide us with a calm oasis of physical comfort and emotional healing.

Sleeping Out

Beds in many ancient cultures – Egyptian, Greek, Roman, for example – were made of stout linen or rattan woven webbing on a wooden frame and were portable to allow the best choice of breeze or natural lighting/shadow for the sleep or siesta. This principle is still followed in the Middle East, India, Thailand, Indonesia, and even Australia, where many people snooze on the awning-hung veranda or 'sleep-out' on hot summer afternoons or nights. For coolness in the Greek islands people climb up to their stone sleeping platforms, where a pile of mattresses is laid out, sometimes with a sperveri cone-shaped embroidered curtain enclosing the 'bed' to keep out mosquitoes and other insects. Good circulation of air, soothing diffused natural light (natural cheesecloth or calico drapes or linen blinds are perfect), and an erasure of harsh noise are all requirements of a rewarding daytime nap. Sound-proofing may indeed cut out the drone and roar of the traffic, but sadly also it muffles such magically sleep-inducing sounds as falling rain and trees rustling in the wind. Louvered wooden shutters such as are universally used in Spain, France, and Italy are excellent sound and light baffles, while still admitting air to the room.

For beautiful movement in material in the bedroom, of course one has to choose something natural and lightweight (possibly tropical-style cheesecloth, silk, or light linen) in generous proportions. Soft, giant drapes swirling in a brisk evening zephyr are an eloquent frame to any threshold between your sanctum and the endlessly changing weather patterns of the outside world. If the weather is hot why not just resort to a good oldfashioned fan: either a whirling colonial ceiling job; a Chandleresque desk fan; or the flat paddle-shaped utilitarian hand-held whisks favored by old ladies in Chinatown.

Daybeds for Daydreaming

Very smart do-it-yourself daybeds can be manufactured from old recycled children's cribs with one set of side-bars removed, a lick of paint applied (Olive/Old white/Gustavian blue/New England red), and deluged with soft, plump pillows made from romantically faded reclaimed fabric. Alternatively drape an old divan with some sumptuous old curtaining, make a corona out of an antique-style light fitting and attach it over the divan with some filmy voile swooping down from it on each side. There you have it: a blissfully romantic Regency daybed for comfy

For a truly informal siesta cool cotton hammocks can be hung on balconies, verandas, or between two gnarled old apple trees in an orchard garden. This one is slung between terrace roof supports in a house on the island of Lamu, East Africa.

naps, convalescence, or canoodling. If you fancy the mystical feel of a transparent tent, just pull your voile right around the bed. If more shade is required in your bosky nautically inspired slumber-spot create an *ad hoc* tent with a couple of cunningly draped sheets, or, for a really ethereal atmosphere, an old silk parachute from an army surplus store.

It is sometimes difficult in small apartments to achieve the sense of withdrawal for private thoughts and energy renewal that the concept 'bedroom' represents. In studio rooms and converted high-ceilinged loft spaces with balcony-bedrooms, a notional sense of separate space can be created by hanging embroidered, beaded, or sequinned transparent saris from the ceiling to the balcony rail, like brilliant-hued billowing medieval banners. Rattan or bamboo hanging baskets full of interesting and unusual indoor plants with a jungly look can also do the same job.

Objects for Special Focus

Position special objects of visual delight such as beautiful stones or sculpture, children's pictures, family photos, or flowers that you love in positions where you will see them as soon as you open your eyes. Under no circumstances have a telephone or television in the bedroom, for their very presence proffers an invitation not to doze, read, or pay attention to your partner! The low-level electromagnetic field pollution emitted by television transmitters is best avoided by those trying to create a health-giving, stress-free sanctum. A far better way to invite refreshing repose is to position your bed opposite a window with a view of trees (if you haven't got one, paint one!), or underneath a skylight where you can gaze up at the scintillating wonders of the night sky. *Feng shui* experts say it is best not to position bedroom mirrors opposite windows or doors or the incoming energy flow will be disturbed. Mirrors opposite beds are also taboo because their perceived powers of energy reflection are thought to disturb sleep patterns and cause nightmares.

Eclectic combinations of stark purity of form and fantastically ornate ornamentation, severe modernism, and antiques from all eras, can work very well in your room of dreams. The paradox of these differing design styles provides corners of visual intrigue and sensibility stimulation.

A Natural Look

Many people, however, prefer a more tranquil, monastic style or the austerely simple bedroom look favored in traditional Japanese home style, with foldaway futon beds, tatami mats, and removable paper screens the only signifiers of room divisions and separate bed-space. At least allow yourself an 'altar' table or tokonama shrine-alcove in which to display some personally meaningful image or beautiful object/s. If natural, 'found' objects are what you are drawn to, make a mobile of gathered sticks, stones and shells, plus personally meaningful icons and images (a departed friend, a zodiac sign, an animal totem). These all go toward meeting our deep desire to communicate directly with the powers and intensities of the natural world.

Translucent, softly luminous, washes of wall color in misty mauves (violet is traditionally calming and spiritually uplifting) or mystical chalky blues combine with elegantly simple unbleached linen materials and look very restful (both hues are sedative to the nervous system), in both bright natural daytime direct light and indirect artificial light. A mirror ball or mobile of crystals hanging near the window to catch the sunlight can produce a prismatic rainbow of refracted colors to dance around the room.

Colors for Luck

Chinese mystical belief holds that some colors are good-luck enhancers, and it is always advisable to attract good luck to the bedroom. Bedrooms conducive to marital harmony should have an interplay of yin (light, female) and yang (dark, male) hues, with pinks a particularly auspicious grade of tint because they are in the sensual, energizing red (fire) color family. Green, the color associated with growth, fruitfulness, and health, is thought to be a good partner for bedroom pinks, as is pale blue, which symbolizes hope.

Indian bedroom esthetics were set down in an ancient courtly text called the *Shilpa Shastra*, which recommends, for example, red and gold to embody passion and opulence, and lime green to represent developing love.

Spirituality and Sexuality

The noncompartmentalized everyday sensuality of the fifth-century Hindu Sanskrit sex manual the *Kama Sutra* does not separate spirituality and sexuality at all. Amatory participants are advised to read the Sanskrit Vedas in between following the example of Kama, the Indian god of erotic love. This 'holy sex' tradition began with the third-century Indian religion of Tantra, which saw sexual union as a cosmic event in which the male represented the god Shiva, and the woman a Shakti goddess. Tantric 'sacred sex' teachers advise that before further intimacies partners look into each other's left eye (this eye being 'the window of the soul'), while keeping a hand on each other's heart.

Favored Aphrodisiacs

Every culture has had its favored aphrodisiacs (the word comes from Aphrodite, the Greek incarnation of an all-powerful ancient fertility goddess). The Aztecs were partial to the avocado, while the Ancient Egyptians got themselves in the mood with lettuce and radish, and the Roman poet Ovid recommended devour-

Among the leisured classes in days of yore *chaises-longues* and daybeds, the latter often modeled on the French *lit bateau* (boat-shaped bed), were dotted about the house for those who fancied forty winks after a heavy lunch. Traditionally the pillows at either end of a daybed are giant bolsters. This is a bedroom in an 18th-century Provençal farmhouse (overleaf).

ing onions! Mexicans have always sworn by vanilla pods steeped in hot chocolate. The Italian serial philanderer Casanova reputedly devoured 50 oysters every morning for breakfast before looking for conquests. On a less challenging note, pot-pourri or 'love-pillows' containing a high proportion of dried verbena leaves are old English olfactory erotic stimulants, as are sheets scented with woodruff, lavender, marjoram, or spearmint (which Culpeper describes as stirring up 'venery or bodily lust'). Many people, however, rely on a warm destressing bath followed by a mutual massage with exotically aromatic ylang-ylang, rose, or jasmine essential oil, as a forefunner to more intimate bedroom bliss.

A Good Mattress

Whatever the look of your bedroom surroundings or your taste in love techniques and potions, it is essential for good sleep and comfortable relaxation, passive and active (for many people read, draw, and doodle down ideas in bed, apart from anything else), to invest in an excellent mattress. In the past people have stuffed their mattresses with dried leaves, scented grasses (such as ladies' bedstraw), heather, feathers, animal hair, and wild flowers. These days, though, natural fibers and a resilient inner spring are desirable qualities in a mattress, which, when resting on a craftsman-made slatted wooden base, should provide comfy but firm support for your spine.

Advised Bedding

Soft yet supportive pure wool fiber-filled under-quilts and pillows are available for people who suffer from backache, rheumatism, and muscular problems. Pure unbleached linen or cotton sheets, and a down-soft traditional Kashmiri summer blanket (hand-washed in icy streams and then beaten against rocks to make them downy and supple) would be the ultimate luxury for warm season bedtimes. Avoid synthetic materials that induce sweating and static electricity. For winter old-fashioned eiderdowns look more characterful and are more snuggly than comforters … refurbished ones are increasingly turning up in chichi antique stores, but you can still pick the odd one up at garage/rummage sales. If the feathers have matted together, with age, it is possible to restuff with new ones.

Quilts as Art

Apart from their decorative value as intricate kaleidoscopes of color, hand-stitched quilts are often commemorative works of art, not only in their pictorial depiction but also because each scrap used is usually a piece of special fabric with nostalgic value – a fragment of mother's favorite rosy velvet curtains, for example, sewn in a pattern next to a treasured snip of daughter's

This asymmetric four-poster, decorated with evocative shells and fruit, made for an English house high on a hill in Bristol, has been fashioned out of recycled unmatched table legs and old stair bannisters.

first floral-sprigged cotton romper suit and a patch cut from that silk ballgown or denim dungarees you were wearing when he proposed.

The generational age-difference between the scraps of material gives a quilt a sense of historical continuum and creative representation of family bonding through the decades and centuries.

The most valuable of all quilts for the serious collector are the geometric works of art made by the reclusive American Mennonite sect, the Amish, who made each one with a deliberate mistake, to highlight human imperfection. To make your own ornamental bedcover you don't have to be brilliant at hand sewing. Luckily these days primitive-style stitchery is in fashion! Use a combination of materials you love, and either sew on motifs, runes, and symbols which are important to you (spirals are old Celtic signs for male and female energy, for example), or you could just use material paint. You could continue the theme on the curtains and/or armoire-cupboards, chests of drawers, and trunks. If you don't feel confident with freehand, use découpage cut, paste, and varnish techniques to add stars, moons, flowers, birds, butterflies … whatever takes your fancy.

Enhance the bower atmosphere with decorative seasonal foliage or scented flowers (roses, narcissi, lilies, hyacinths) artlessly spilling from a variety of characterful containers, old and new. Even in a poky inner city guestroom, a visitor greeted by the color and scent of a thoughtful floral offering will feel linked to the complex beauty of the great outdoors. Bring color and texture inside in the form of armfuls of flowers. Match tall, creamy lilies and white daisies with the natural palette of terra-cotta and stone; set watercolor-hued violets and rosebuds against a pale, dreamy wall, or go for warmth and dramatic surprise with bright red geraniums or scarlet and black anemones against the dappled sunlight reflected on the bedspread.

And So, To Bed

Your dream bed might be rugged American country cherrywood, antique carved Indonesian, ornate iron four-poster, or English Victorian brass, but the status or look of the furniture does not, of course, guarantee a good night's sleep.

There have been many recipes and remedies over the centuries for insomnia … for as research has shown, one in three adults has problems with either falling asleep in the first place or with staying asleep and that people tend to sleep better in a bigger bed, with or without counting sheep. Visualizing wandering along in the haven of your perfect dream garden on soft grass in bare feet, slowly but rhythmically inhaling the celestial scent of the flowers, is a tried and true sleep invitation.

This minimalist attic bedroom in a London apartment was inspired by Japanese designs and makes effective use of natural light and shadow. The walls were stripped and horizontal beams removed; weight redistributed to the four corners. The wall cladding is basic, cheap wall paneling.

Sleep Aromas

The Elizabethan physician John Gerard was convinced that aroma was the secret of a good night's sleep: 'The distilled water of roses … bringeth sleep, which also the fresh roses themselves provoke through their sweet and pleasant smell'. Dream that you are reclining on a bed of roses by using a medieval-style 'casting bottle' (a large sugar or salt shaker is a good facsimile), full of rosewater or water and a few drops of oil of attar of roses (very expensive), or rosewood or rose geranium … sprinkle a few drops around when you are airing the bedding. *The Queen's Delight*, 1662, has a tempting suggestion for 'An Odiferous Perfume for Chambers': 'Take a glasseful of Rose Water, Cloves well beaten to powdcr, a penny weight; then take the fine panne and make it red hot in the fyre, and put thereon of the said Rose water with the sayd pouder of Cloves making it so consume … and you shall make a perfume of excellent good odour.'

Lavender, which herbalist John Parkinson said was of 'especiall good use for all griefs and paines of the head and braine', used to be used in Europe to stuff padded winter nightcaps. A big bowl of lavender heads, enlivened occasionally with essential oil of lavender, placed on or near the bedside table, probably does the sleep-inducing job just as well. It is also a calming restorative for those who are merely fatigued and need a brief rest before rejoining the fray. Those needing a rather sensuous sort of rest should stir their lavender with a twig from the hawthorn, pagan symbol of fertility. On a more sedate note, lavender tea served with a little honey, a favorite with 'delicate' ladies in Victorian times, is a delicious and effective companion to repose.

In Europe and the United States up until the early twentieth century country sleep pillows were made from herbs and gently narcotic hops … a tradition dating back to aristocratic women of medieval times and their harvests from household physic gardens.

These somnolent botanical delights are relatively easy to make … you can adapt the cover and contents to suit each member of the family or room (they are perfect accessories for sofas and daybeds, too). Silk taffeta and silk brocade make a regal sleep-pillow envelope … look around the remaindered off-cuts for small amounts of appropriately lavish fabrics. Use cheesecloth, unbleached calico, or large cotton handkerchiefs for the inner lining. The following warm and wistful mixture, 'Parisian Pillow of Hopeful Dreams', features marjoram, a herb sacred to the goddess of love, Aphrodite. Mix well before placing inside the inner lining, enlarge the proportions for a bigger pillow: one cup of dried hops; one cup of small deep-red scented dried rosebuds; one and a half cups of dried mar-

Few things are more atmospheric to cover the bed during the daytime than a hand-made quilt, be it an exquisite family heirloom or a quaint folksy junk-store find made from someone else's fascinating ragbag scraps. In this small, cozy bedroom in a London apartment, the red walls complement the warm quilt colors.

147

joram flowers; a half cup of dried rosemary; a quarter of a cup of dried orris root powder; five drops of petitgrain essential oil; five drops of rose geranium essential oil; and two drops of bergamot essential oil.

If you want to refresh your sheets and towels while they are resting in the linen cupboard try making these sweet scented bags, from *The Art of Cookery* by Mrs Hannah Glasse, 1784, to lay between the folds: eight ounces of damask rose leaves (petals), eight ounces of coriander seeds, eight ounces of sweet orris-root, eight ounces of *calamus aromaticus*, one ounce of mace, one ounce of cinnamon, half an ounce of cloves, four drachms of musk powder, two drachms of white loaf sugar, three ounces of lavender flowers and some Rhodium wood. Beat them well together and make them in small silk bags.'

Aromas for Convalescence

Those convalescing could benefit from the room being sprayed with a plant mister to which half a dozen drops of lavender oil or disinfectant rosemary (from 'ros marinus' – dew of the sea', a herb sacred for many centuries to the Virgin Mary) had been added. Indeed, right back in Anglo-Saxon times, an old herbal manuscript advised: 'For the sickly take this wort rosemary, pound it with oil, smear the sickly one, wonderfully thou healest him'.

We must speak now of those who are not ill, but sick of heart. Some of the uplifting aromatic essences of nature once used only by the very rich or royal as part of their religious worship are now available to everyone from alternative bookstores and health food stores.

Lifting the Spirits as you Sleep

Those feeling 'low' or troubled with jangled nerves are advised to utilize only genuinely therapeutic incense sticks. For example, those made by the old Indian 'masala' technique, which moulds a 'dough' of aromatic flowers, herbs, resins, leaves, oils, and powders onto a bamboo stick, rather than a synthetic substitute. Guatemalans and other Southern American peoples transfer their anxious thoughts into tiny 'worry dolls', which they keep in brightly colored drawstring bags or boxes under their pillows – possibly knowing full well that in the morning things will seem more positive. These minute dolls are now available in many craft stores and alternative bookstores … teenagers, in particular, find them invaluable! They are also very easy to make yourself, using bendy pipe cleaners wound with brightly colored scraps of knitting wool.

Some people believe that certain gemstones have healing and mood-enhancing energies. Moonstones, opalescent formations used as magic charms affecting well-being since very early times, we mentioned earlier (see p.132). In the metaphys-

These children's bunks are squeezed into a tiny space on a houseboat moored on the River Thames at Kew, London. A porthole reveals that most of this bedroom is situated well below the water line.

ical Indian system of human energy fields, or chakras, the seventh chakra at the crown of the head governs the pineal gland (described by the writer H. P. Lovecraft as the 'sense organ of the mind'). Sodalite is a much-favored stone traditionally associated both with the pineal gland and with spiritual enlightenment.

A Child's Room

A child's bedroom should be a bright and happy place – safe and stimulating, with natural-fiber matting and materials, and nonpetrochemical-based paintwork. Maximize space by making your older child a platform bed (painted to resemble a castle, or pirate ship, perhaps), with useful cupboard space underneath.

For less rough-and-tumble-oriented kids, even an ordinary bed can be turned into a special retreat and play-den with the addition of mosquito-net-type curtaining hung from the ceiling. Sew sequins or bugle-beads here and there to glitter and gleam in the sunlight or starrily by the glow of the (safe, battery-operated) night-light. A cuddly bed quilt and/or blanket inspiring much conversation and nostalgia can be made from your child's old baby-dresses, romper suits, and woolens.

Tinies' Textures and Textiles

Organic cotton materials using natural dyes that don't use heavy metals are the ideal choice for babies' and young children's clothes and bedding, as is wool when it is produced to strict eco-standards and is free of chemi-

cal residues. All children enjoy the sensory experience of different textures – make up a patchwork playmat or crib lining using materials with varying soft and rough(ish) finishes. Put little pockets all over them housing small material people in 'sleeping-bags'. It's a good idea for the nursery itself to be either relatively plain in decoration to encourage creativity in the child … all drawings, collages, and other artistic efforts should be proudly displayed; or painted with an imaginative mural, some of the nicest ones feature family members and pets, with spaces for the child to later paint in friends and favorite toys.

Cradles for Rocking

The best bed of all for a very little baby is an old-fashioned rocking cradle … the combination of slow rocking and a hummed lullaby is a tried and true sleep recipe. The Shakers even made grown-up-size ones for sick and elderly adults in their communities, such was their belief in the healing power of rocking. In Europe in centuries past rocking cradles were traditionally made of oak, a pagan protective tree, and hung with anti-evil-eye amulets of magical rowan or hawthorn, emblems of fertility, birth, and child protection … tied with anti-witchcraft red thread. Cedar is another wood with links to children … cedar incense is traditionally used by some Native American peoples at child blessing ceremonies.

A charming baby's crib mobile can be made from one or all of the above-mentioned 'sacred' woods (carefully rubbed down so that no pieces of bark or splinters will drop off), with feathers, holed stones, and spirals of colored paper firmly tied on with red ribbon.

In addition, a small sprig of fresh lavender or eucalypt tied on will help keep flies and germs at bay. Small children love looking at pictures of themselves … make copies of lots of photos of them with family, friends, toys, fictional characters, and pets and use the resulting collage varnished with a safe resin-based eco-varnish to cover a small tea table or playbox. Make a miniature window-garden of bulbs so that the little ones (above the age of eating them!), can observe firsthand the curious daily changes of nature.

Children's Sleeplessness

Sleeplessness in children can often be cured with the soothing ritual of a warm drink, a comforting bedtime story, and a dab of 'Magic Dreamcream'. Mine consists of bland, unperfumed aqueous cream from the drug store put into a tiny fairy-sized pot with the addition of a drop each of lavender, rose, and camomile essential oil. Make a Native American 'dream-catcher' to hang over your child's bed.

Shaped like a small spider's web on a stick and bedecked with shells, beads, and feathers, these mystical implements were traditionally tied to the side of a baby-carrying papoose or hung over the child's bed in the tipi to keep nightmares at bay. You could also make a child-sized sleep pillow in washable cotton with a sturdy lining to ensure no wispy bits of herb poke through.

Camomile is a traditionally soothing child's herb … three or four drops in water in a plant mister makes a lovely child's room freshener. However, never spray anything near a small baby's face, and remember that essential oils should be stored safely out of the reach of small children as they are highly toxic if swallowed.

Put this delicately aromatic and soporific mixture for the over-threes into a cloth bag before putting it into a star-decorated pillowcase with plenty of padding. You can make the stars using material cut-outs or potato prints. Take two cups of camomile flowers, one cup of dried lavender flowers, one cup of strongly scented dried rose petals, a quarter of a cup of orrisroot powder, two finely crushed cloves, and two drops of camomile essential oil. Mix the ingredients thoroughly before using.

'We are such stuff as dreams are made on …'
The Tempest, William Shakespeare

resources

suppliers

When writing to any of the following, please enclose a stamped, addressed envelope to ensure a reply.

PAINTS AND WALLCOVERINGS

Factory Paint Store
505 Pond Street
S. Weymouth, MA 02190
(781) 331-1200
www.gis.net/~fps/index.htm
A collection of unique wallcoverings and paint supplies. Catalog available.

HERBS & POTPOURRI

Gardener's Supply Co.
128 Intervale Road
Dept PR97
Burlington, VT 05401-2850
(800) 955-3370
A variety of dried and fresh herbs and gardening tools and materials, many unusual or hard-to-find. Catalog available.

East Earth
(800) 258-6878
www.snowcres.net/eetw/
A fine variety of Chinese herbs. Offer an extensive range of rare herbs, informative books, green tea, and prepared herbal remedies. Catalog available.

The Healthy Trader
(800) 636-2584
Herbal & medicinal teas and organic, sulfite-free wines. Catalog available.

OILS & SOAPS

Burt's Bees
(800) 849-7112
Over ninety earth-friendly, natural personal care products to choose from, including soaps, bath oils, powders, bath salts, salves, creams, many made with honey. Catalog available.

Maine Mountain Soap & Candle Company
(800) 287-2141
e-mail: MaineMtn@aol.com
Small company producing quality handmade, natural candles and bath products. Catalog available.

Neal's Yard Apothecary
St. James' House
John Dalton Street
Manchester
England
Dried herbs, pure soaps, aromatherapy kits and ceramic burners and make-your-own toiletry ingredients. Available in some American department stores, or write for a catalog.

The Essential Oil Company
(800) 729-5912
Pure aromatherapy-grade essential oils and supplies for making your own bath products at home. Catalog available.

Earth Harmony
(800) 341-2604
A large selection of premium pure essential oils, imported from around the world. They also offer a collection of beautiful aromatherapy accessories includes soaking salts, blends, eye pillows, books, massage oils, diffusers and more. Catalog available.

CANDLES AND LIGHTING

Arte De Mexico
(818) 508-0993
A collection of authentic hand-crafted Moroccan lighting. Made in Morocco by Nomadic tribesmen in the traditional manner; intricate detail and brightly colored glass make each piece truly unique. Call for information.

River Road Traditions
RR#3 Port Elgin
Ontario
CANADA
NOH 2C7
Ph/Fax: (519) 389-3916
1-800-263-8938
www.bmts.com/~rrt
Handcrafted period lighting, tinware, period home accessories and unique gifts for the home. Catalog available.

RUGS & FLOORCOVERINGS

Antique Rug Studio
(212) 753-9490
Large selections of fine antique European carpets. Call for information.

Damoka USA Inc.
(212) 213-1500
A large selection of Oriental and European decorative and antique carpets and period tapestries from early 19th through early 20th century. Specializes in over-sized and unusual carpets. Call for information.

Country Floors
(212) 627-8300
15 East 16th Street
New York, NY 10003
An extensive and beautiful selection of tiles for walls and floors from around the world. Many hard-to-find, one-of-a-kind and antique tiles, as well as

contemporary and simple ceramics. Catalog available, showroom open to the public.

NEW AGE MUSIC

New World Aurora
16A Neal's Yard
London WC2H
England
Mecca for crystal seekers, as well as a stimulating source of New Age ambient music, Gregorian chants, Celtic songs, Native American music. Mail order for music on 171 198 681 1682

Heaven & Earth
RR1 Box 25
Marshfield, VT 05658
(800) 348-5155
(802) 426-3440
A large selection of New Age and spiritual music on tape and CD. Catalog available.

FURNITURE & ANTIQUES

Kim 3 - 18th and 19th century
(310) 859-3844
Chinese antiques, 16th and 17th Tibetan antiques, large selection of Indonesian furniture and accessories. Call for information.

Liza Hyde Antique Japanese Screens
(212) 752-3581
Internationally known dealer in Japanese screens of all periods, subjects and price points. Call for information.

Tobias & The Angel
6-8 White Hart Lane
London SW13 OPZ
England
Rustic antique furniture and household goods plus decorative objects made from recycled fabrics and oddments.

Antique gardening utensils. Write for information.

Solar Antique Tiles
(212) 755-2403
www.solarantiquetiles.com
Antique tiles from the palaces and estates of Europe. Hand-painted murals dating from as far back as the 1500s to as recently as the 1930s. Available through decorators, but call or e-mail for information.

BEDDING

Cuddledown of Maine
(800) 323-6793
Extraordinary selection of down comforters and pillows. Bedding ensembles in cotton, linen and silk; sleepwear, hand-carved beds, tables, custom-sewn bedding ensembles. Excellent quality. Catalog available.

The Company Store
(800) 285-3696
Large selection of cotton and down comforters, duvet covers, wool and down pillows, blankets, sheets and bedroom accessories. Catalog available.

GENERAL

ABC Carpet & Home
(212) 473-3000
www.abchome.com
A large collection of antique and new furniture, rugs, china, glassware, fabric, gifts and accessories for the home. Five floors, plus a "bargain basement" and a café. When visiting New York City, it's an essential stop on any itinerary. Occasional floor sample sales offer good-value large furniture. Call ahead first.

D.W. Rosas
27176 Shadowcrest Ln. Ste 100
Cathedral City
CA 92234
(760) 322-7268
www.dwrosas.com
Decorative accessory and furniture design company specializing in unique hand-painted finished accessories. Call or e-mail for information.

Chintz & Company
1720 Store St.
Victoria
BC. V8W 1V5
(250) 381-2404
www.chintz.com
An emporium of imported textiles, furniture, dishes, exotic mulberry paper flowers, antique garden statues, soaps and oils, books and home accessories. Call or e-mail.

Red Rose Collection
826 Burlway
Burlingame
CA 94010
(800) 220-ROSE
A variety of home accessories, gifts, and unique art, including sculpture and paintings. Catalog available.

The Mill Outlet
7605 Coastal Highway
Ocean City
MD 21842
410-524-6644
Toll Free: 888-207-3052
www.milloutlet.com
Complete selection of top-quality home textiles including sheets, jersey knit sheets, bedspreads, comforters, beach towels, bathroom ensembles, table linens, bedding accessories and more. In addition, they carry a large assortment of unique giftware and lamps. Catalog available.

RESOURCES

bibliography

Earth to Spirit – In Search of Natural Architecture David Pearson, Chronicle, 1994.

Shaker Built Paul Rocheleau, June Sprigg, David Larkin, Thames and Hudson, 1994.

The Natural House Book David Pearson, Simon & Schuster, 1989.

Natural Housekeeping Beverly Pagram, Trafalgar Square, 1997.

The Mind's Eye: Imagery in Everyday Life Robert Sommer, Dell, New York, 1978.

The Earth Spirit – Its Ways, Shrines and Mysteries John Michell, Thames and Hudson, 1975.

The Mystic Spiral Jill Purce, Thames and Hudson, 1974.

The Eye – The Seer and the Seen Francis Huxley, Thames and Hudson, 1990.

The Illustrated Book of Signs and Symbols Miranda Bruce-Mitford, Dorling Kindersley, 1996.

Images of Power - Aboriginal Art of the Kimberley Judith Ryan and Kim Ackerman, National Gallery of Victoria, 1993.

Where Every Breath is a Prayer Jon Ortner, Stewart, Tabori and Chang, New York, 1996.

North American Mythology Cottie Burland, rev. Marion Wood, Newnes Books, 1965.

The Elements of Native American Traditions Arthur Versluis, Element, 1993.

Dictionary of World Folklore Larousse, 1995.

The Dictionary of Festivals The Aquarian Press, 1990.

The Mammoth Book of Ancient Wisdom Cassandra Eason, Robinson, 1997.

Sacred Space Denise Linn, Rider, 1995.

Chakras For Beginners Naomi Ozaniec, Headline, 1994.

Living Color Master Lin Yun, Kodansha International, New York, 1994.

Pleasures of the Japanese Bath, Peter Grilli & Dana Levy, Weatherhill, New York/Tokyo, 1992.

Feng Shui Handbook, Master Lam Kam Chuen, Henry Holt, 1995.

Personal Feng Shui, Master Lam Kam Chuen, Henry Holt, 1998

Islamic Art Barbara Brend, British Museum Press, 1991.

Casa Mexicana Tim Street-Porter, Stewart, Tabori and Chang, 1989.

Ethnic Style Miranda Innes, Conran Octopus, 1991.

Pure Style Jane Cumberbatch, Ryland, Peters & Small, 1996.

Trade Secrets Jocasta Innes, Weidenfeld and Nicolson, 1995.

Tricia Guild's Painted Country Nonie Nieswand, Conran Octopus, 1994.

African Designs Rebecca Jewell, British Museum Press, 1994.

Decorative Arts of the Amish of Lancaster County Daniel and Kathryn McCauley, Good Books, Pennsylvania, 1988.

The Art of the Maze Adrian Fisher & Georg Gerster, Weidenfeld and Nicolson, 1990.

The Art of Pebble Mosaics Maggy Howarth, Search Press, 1994.

Creative Vegetable Gardening, Joy Larkom, Mitchell Beazley, 1997.

Water Features For Small Gardens Francesca Greenoak, Conran Octopus, 1996.

The Scented Garden Rosemary Verey, Michael Joseph, 1981.

Derek Jarman's Garden Derek Jarman, Thames and Hudson, 1995.

The Inward Garden - Creating A Place of Beauty and Meaning Julie Moir Messervy, Little, Brown, New York, 1995.

The History and Religion of the Great Islamic Gardens Meredith Press, New York, 1987.

Tree Medicine Tree Magic, Ellen Evert Hopman, Phoenix Pulbishing, Washington, 1991.

Heirloom Herbs Mary Forsell, Villard Books, New York, 1990.

Potpourris and Other Fragrant Delights Jacqueline Hériteau, Penguin, 1975.

A Modern Herbal Mrs M. Grieve, Jonathan Cape, 1931 (reprinted Tiger Books, 1992).

index

Bold numerals refer to main text entries; *italic* numerals refer to photographs or captions.

picture credits

Iain Bagwell: p.75, pp.96-7

Bridgeman Art Library London: Musee d'Orsay, 'The Meal (The Bananas)', Paul Gauguin, 1891, p.7, pp.59 -9; Private Collection, Peter Willi, 'Landscape With a Dog in Front of a Shed', Paul Gauguin, 1892, p.6, p.12

Hotze Eisma: pp.92-3, pp.134-35

Robert Harding Syndication: Andreas von Einsiedel, *Homes & Gardens* front cover; Christopher Drake, *Homes & Gardens* p.99; Fritz von der Schulenburg, *Country Homes & Interiors p.*81; Jan Baldwin p.73; Jan Baldwin, *Homes & Gardens* p.145; John Miller,*Casa* p.15, p.19; John Miller, *Villa* p.65; Polly Wreford, *Homes & Gardens* p.125; Simon Upton, *Country Homes & Interiors* pp.102-103; Trevor Richard, *Homes & Gardens* p.114

The Interior Archive: Cecilia Innes p.84, p.106, p.133; Christopher Simon Sykes p.49, p.61, p.130; Fritz von der Schulenburg p.4, half-title, p.18, p.23, p.24, p.62, p.76, p.90, p.95, pp.116-17, p.123, p.137, p.149; Jacques Dirand pp.140-41; Simon Brown p.146; Tim Beddow p.25, pp.78-9; Nadia Mackenzie p.143

Elizabeth Whiting & Associates: Andreas von Einsiedel p.108; Brian Harrison p.126; Dennis Stone p.68, p.100; Jean-Paul Bonhommet p.50, pp.70-71; Michael Dunne pp.88-9; Nadia Mackenzie p.28, pp.120-21; Peter Aprahamian p.67; Peter Wolosznski p.11; Tim Street-Porter p.111; Tom Leighton p.22, p.105

author's acknowledgments

The author wishes to thank the following people for their help and support during the creation of the book: Jonathan, Orlanda and Morwenna Baylis for being understanding during long working hours; plus Jo Godfrey Wood and Sara Mathews at Gaia for putting the project together so imaginatively.

publisher's acknowledgments

Gaia Books would like to thank the following for their assistance in the production of this book: Lynn Bresler (index and proofreading), Erica Kelly (location) and Beverly LeBlanc.